Business Ethics

Business Ethics
A Kantian Perspective

Norman E. Bowie

BLACKWELL
Publishers

Extracts from *Constructions of Reason* by Onora O'Neill are reprinted with the permission of Cambridge University Press and the author.

Extracts from *Creating the Kingdom of Ends* by Christine Korsgaard are reprinted with the permission of Cambridge University Press and the author.

Extracts from Immanuel Kant's *Foundations of the Metaphysics of Morals*, translated by L.W. Beck, are reprinted by permission of Prentice-Hall, Inc., Upper Saddle River, NJ, USA.

W. Ouchi, *Theory Z*, © 1981 by Addison Wesley Publishing Company, Inc. Reprinted by permission of Addison Wesley Longman.

Extracts from *Trust: The Social Virtues and the Creation of Prosperity* by Francis Fukuyama are reprinted with the permission of The Free Press, a Division of Simon & Schuster. Copyright © 1995 by Francis Fukuyama.

First published 1999

2 4 6 8 10 9 7 5 3 1

Blackwell Publishers Inc.
350 Main Street
Malden, Massachusetts 02148
USA

Blackwell Publishers Ltd
108 Cowley Road
Oxford OX4 1JF
UK

Library of Congress Cataloging-in-Publication Data
Bowie, Norman E., 1942–
Business ethics: a Kantian perspective / Norman E. Bowie.
p. cm.
Includes bibliographical references and index.
ISBN 0-631-21173-X. – ISBN 0-631-21174-8 (pbk.)
1. Business ethics. I. Title.
HF5387.B683 1999
174'.4 – dc21 98-28676
CIP

British Library Cataloguing in Publication Data

A CIP catalogue record for this book is available from the British Library

Typeset in 11 on 13 pt Bembo
by Best-set Typesetter Ltd., Hong Kong
Printed in Great Britain by M.P.G. Books, Bodmin, Cornwall

This book is printed on acid-free paper

Contents

Preface

This book is the culmination of five years of research, discussion, and rewriting. It began in 1994 with an invitation to present a Ruffin lecture at the Darden School, University of Virginia. I decided to write on Kantian capitalism because my friend Ed Freeman had not completed that project himself. His essay with William Evan published in the third edition of Beauchamp and Bowie's *Ethical Theory and Business* was entitled "A Stakeholder Theory of the Modern Corporation: Kantian Capitalism." However, Ed's stakeholder theory has taken a more pragmatic turn so I decided to try to develop the Kantian line. Although I cannot recall all the names of all the people who provided comments at the lecture, several people provided helpful written comments including Robert Frederick, William Frederick, Richard De George, Edwin Hartman, and Andy Wicks.

I then presented the paper on two occasions at the Carlson School of Management at the University of Minnesota. On this occasion I received a number of helpful comments from faculty and graduate students including Kathryn Brewer, the late Larry Cummings, Geoff Bell, Bryan Frances, and Tanya Kostova.

I decided to turn the paper into a book. I was fortunate to receive a fellowship in the Program in Ethics and the Professions at Harvard in 1996–7. Thus, I was able to spend my sabbatical writing the book. I am deeply indebted to the members of the seminar that year: Dennis Thompson, Arthur Applbaum, Larry Lessig, Arti Rai, Tom Sorrell, Carol Steiker, and Melissa S. Williams for their helpful comments on what turned out to be chapter 3. I am especially

indebted to Tom Sorrell, who read the entire manuscript and
provided detailed comments on every chapter. Others who read the
manuscript in whole or in part include Deborah Cohen, Deborah
Johnson, Ellen Klein, David Newell, Richard Nielsen, Scott
Reynolds, Richard Parker, Jeffrey Smith, Edward Soule, Kathleen
Sutcliffe, Alec Waldren, and Patricia Werhane.

Finally, I thank the University of Minnesota for granting me the
sabbatical leave which enabled me to finish the book. I also thank
my wife Maureen who traveled with me to Cambridge for the
sabbatical and has provided encouragement and inspiration all the
way.

Norman Bowie
Minneapolis, March 1998

Introduction

This book is an attempt to apply the essential features of Kantian moral philosophy to the business firm. More specifically, it addresses the question, "How would a business firm in a capitalist economy be structured and managed according to the principles of Kant's ethics?" I shall use Kant's three formulations of the categorical imperative to answer that question. Each of the next three chapters uses one of the three formulations of the categorical imperative as its organizing theme. In chapter 4 I note that business leaders often point out that by taking the moral high road they can increase profits. I then discuss whether that recognition on the part of business leaders nullifies the morality of what they have done; after all, Kant insists that a genuine moral act must be done out of duty and not merely in conformity with duty. Finally, in chapter 5, I trace out some of the implications of Kant's cosmopolitanism for international management.

In chapter 1 I shall briefly argue that Kant's first formulation of the categorical imperative provides a theory of moral permissibility for market interactions. Interactions that violate the universalizability formulation of the categorical imperative are morally impermissible. Interactions that are consistent with the universalizability formulation are permissible so long as they do not violate any other moral principles. The second formulation of the categorical imperative – the respect for humanity in persons formulation – provides the basis for a more robust theory of moral obligation in personal market interactions. At a minimum, labor cannot be treated as a commodity like land, money, and machines. All persons in a market transaction

must be treated with respect. Business firms have a perfect obligation to neither coerce nor deceive corporate stakeholders. Respecting the humanity in persons involves imperfect duties as well. In
Chapter 2 I argue that business firms have an imperfect duty to
provide their employees with meaningful work. The argument for
this contention is supported by both the respect for persons formulation of the categorical imperative and by other material from
Kant's writings on ethics. The third formulation of the categorical
imperative, which I shall call the moral community formulation,
provides the foundation for a moral business organization and is the
focus of chapter 3.[1] In chapter 3 I evaluate traditional corporate
structures and incentives. Since most traditional structural forms will
fail the test of Kantian morality, I argue that Kantian moral philosophy requires greater democratization of the workplace.

In all three chapters I provide examples of how behaving morally
can contribute to profitability. However, I argue in chapter 4 that
recognition of that fact need not violate Kant's dictum that genuinely moral action must be done from the motive of duty (because
it is right). Lastly, in chapter 5 I contend that Kant's general
Enlightenment moral position supports the goal of an international
business community free of war and particularist strife, be it religious, ethnic, or nationalistic. Business adherence to Enlightenment
ideals will enable business to play a positive role in building a moral
world community. Such optimism is characteristic of Enlightenment
thought.

Several caveats and clarifications are in order. First, Kant wrote
nothing about capitalism and corporations and little about even
elementary business transactions.[2] In his lectures on ethics which
have come down to us as notes taken by his students, he did speak
on the nature of wealth and on the comparative evils of miserliness
and avarice. We shall explore Kant's thoughts on these matters in
chapter 2.

Second, I believe that empirical knowledge does have an important role to play within Kant's theory. When philosophers and
management professors, who are primarily social scientists, first
began to interact in the Social Issues in Management Division of the
Academy of Management an unfortunate debate erupted around
some comments attributed to business ethicists to the effect that the
facts do not matter in ethical debate. Persons making those remarks

may think they have the support of Kant for their contention. But nothing could be further from the truth. Kant himself was very explicit throughout his philosophical career in pointing out that moral philosophy was mere speculation without the knowledge provided by social science. In the *Lectures on Ethics* Kant is reported to have said:

> Practical philosophy (that is, the science of how man ought to behave) and anthropology (that is, the science of man's actual behavior) are closely connected and the former cannot subsist without the latter; for we cannot tell whether the subject to which our consideration applies is capable of what is demanded of him unless we have knowledge of that subject. It is true that we can pursue the study of practical philosophy without anthropology . . . But our philosophy is then merely speculative and an Idea. We therefore have to make at least some study of man.[3]

It should also be noted that contemporary scholars accept both the fact that Kant knew he needed empirical facts to make moral judgments and that Kant's ethical theory can be applied to issues in the real world. For example, Barbara Herman says flatly, "The *application* of the Moral Law cannot be carried out, however, without empirical knowledge of the object of application."[4] Indeed, Herman specifically applies Kant's theory to condemn the activities of certain cigarette companies that marketed Uptown and Dakota cigarettes to inner-city blacks and "virile females."[5] Thus, I see no theoretical reason not to attempt to show how Kantian moral theory has something significant to say about the prohibition of certain acts in business and about the positive obligations that executives in the business community owe to corporate stakeholders.

Having said this, there is a sense in which the facts do not matter, at least as long as the phrase "do not matter" implies that we should accept the facts as they are. Some findings in organizational behavior are relevant here. Empirical research has shown that contrary to the expectations of equity theory, a statistically significant number of women felt no deprivation when they were paid less than men holding jobs of equal prestige.[6] Apparently the explanation for that phenomenon is that women tend to compare themselves to other women who are also underpaid.[7] In commenting on these findings, Jerald Greenberg said, "To the extent that such norms (differential pay for equal work based on sex) dictate socially acceptable behavior, it is not surprising that women have come to accept as fair the lower pay they receive.[8]

This example of the paradox of the contented female worker illustrates the point behind the philosopher–business ethicist's remarks. The fact that there is a norm that permits paying women less than men for jobs of equal prestige and the fact that women accept it does not make it right. It violates Aristotle's proportionality principle of justice and I would argue that it violates the Kantian moral framework as well. This example provides an important case where the facts do not matter and I trust this case is both obvious and noncontroversial.

Third, although this book refers repeatedly to empirical research that provides evidence or examples for the moral point under discussion, it is in no way a defense of standard business practice. Indeed, I believe that if the Kantian moral perspective in business were taken seriously, business practice would look very different from what it is today. Thus, I am using Kantianism as a theoretical normative framework for telling a story about what a Kantian vision of business organizations would be like. I am not claiming that this is how business practice is; rather, I am providing a vision of what business practice ought to be.

Fourth, although I am not describing capitalism as it is, I do not wish to be considered utopian.[9] I believe a Kantian theory of the modern corporation is possible because it could be workable and profitable. Kant accepted the dictum that "ought implies can." Of course, as a Kantian one would not attempt to reform business because it would be more profitable; one would attempt to reform business because doing so would be the morally right thing to do.

Fifth, I do not believe that the Kantian vision is the only reasonable moral vision that one can apply to business ethics. For example, Robert Solomon has an articulate and inspiring Aristotelian virtue ethics vision.[10] It should not be surprising, after all, that plausible ethical theories give similar answers to what is right and wrong. Thus, utilitarianism, virtue theory, and Kantianism would all condemn failure to keep business contracts or failure to pay one's suppliers. To that extent a person does not have to be a Kantian to accept many of the normative conclusions in this book. Virtue theorists and utilitarians might both agree that profit-sharing plans and open-book management would represent morally better business practice. However, I shall argue later that I believe Kantianism does a better job than competing ethical theories in justifying a number of "good" business practices.

I should also point out that I do not believe that Kantian moral philosophy can address every issue in business ethics. Concerns about the environment were less important in the eighteenth century. Few ethicists at that time, including Kant, were sufficiently sensitive to the suffering of animals. But the fact that the views of ethical theorists are historically situated and thus limited or mistaken in some respects does not mean that we have nothing to learn from them. Aristotle was insensitive to the moral wrong of slavery, but Aristotle still has something to teach us about ethics. More positively, whatever the shortcomings of the Kantian vision, a Kantian theory of the firm has some important insights that the other moral visions of capitalism miss. In other words, a utilitarian or virtue perspective will not be as successful justifying the more participative management practices that would make for more democratic businesses.

I should also note that I do not give a complete analysis of what Kantian moral philosophy would require for all the relations that exist in the corporation. To do so would require a book more than twice the size of this one. For example, I have emphasized the employer–employee relationship in chapters 2 and 3 at the expense of what the second and third formulation of the categorical imperative require for other stakeholder relationships. In addition to the excuse that doing so would make the book too long, I also believe that the contemporary employer–employee relationship is especially morally problematic and thus the focus on that relationship is justified. However, I acknowledge that a complete Kantian theory of the corporation requires additional research both by me and by others who find the Kantian perspective to be fruitful.

Sixth, in writing a book on a Kantian theory of the firm I have tried to be faithful to Kant's ethical theory. I am not simply using Kant where convenient and rejecting him when it is inconvenient. Neither do I reinterpret him so that the Kantian story comes out right. In using Kant's theory I am heavily indebted to four contemporary scholars who have provided interpretive defenses of Kant and I have used their insights in developing my own views on a Kantian theory of the firm. These four contemporary Kant scholars are Barbara Herman, Thomas Hill Jr, Christine Korsgaard, and Onora O'Neill. Although there are significant differences among these four scholars, I believe their interpretations of Kantian ethics make it easier for an applied ethicist to show the relevance of Kant to practical affairs.

Seventh, despite the excellent work of these four Kant scholars, I am well aware that Kantian philosophy is under severe attack. By and large I think that the four scholars mentioned above have defended Kantianism successfully. It is not my intention to contribute to the defense of Kant against his critics. However, a few comments on some specific critiques especially relevant to stands taken in this book require passing comment in this introduction.

For example, some contemporary particularist philosophers have argued that generalizations and moral rules have a relatively minor role to play in ethical decision-making and ethical justification. Two philosophers who hold this view are John McDowell and Jonathan Dancy.[11] Again, contemporary ethicists have challenged these particularist arguments and I have nothing unique to contribute to the debate.[12] However, even if McDowell and Dancy are partially right, this project is not affected. I do not believe that Kantian theory is simply the articulation of a set of absolute rules or principles. My belief on this matter is consistent with contemporary Kant scholarship. Indeed, this exercise in the application of Kantian ethics to the firm will provide further evidence that Kant's ethical theory is far richer than those who view it as a system of rules take it to be.

Over the past 15 years there has been a sustained attack on the impartiality requirement in ethics.[13] This attack has been especially severe with respect to versions of Kantianism. Basically the criticism maintains that relations to friends and family and even countrymen often give those people special status in moral relationships. Kantian morality seems to require that we treat the interests of the stranger as on a par with the interests of a friend.[14] Critics of the impartiality requirement maintain that Kantian morality is mistaken in this respect. Although I think a Kantian may escape that criticism,[15] I shall not argue that point here. Rather, I maintain that if there is a place for the impartiality requirement in ethics, that place is certainly in the ethics of business relationships. Business transactions are supposed to be arms-length transactions. According to the prevailing popular morality, the intrusion of personal interests, such as the interests of family and friends, are inappropriate in most business transactions. To give one's friends or family special consideration in business is often to place oneself in a conflict of interest. It may even put a manager in violation of a fiduciary duty. If these arguments have merit, the critics of impartiality will be less effective against a Kantian theory of business practices than they would be against a Kantian account of morality in general.

Eighth, I am attempting to integrate the insights of Kantian ethics with the insights of management theory, particularly scholarly work in organizational studies. In many business schools there are two competing paradigms for understanding business and business relationships, the economic and the psychological/sociological. Regrettably the economic paradigm which is dominant in finance and accounting has been labeled the hard perspective, while the psychological/sociological perspective – which is very influential in organizational studies, human resources, industrial relations, and strategy – has been labeled the soft perspective. The rationale for the use of the terms "hard" and "soft" is that the mathematical modeling in the economic paradigm is more rigorous and sophisticated. However, as critics in the philosophy of economics point out, that rigor comes at the cost of realism.[16]

Although this work is influenced by both paradigms I am especially indebted to colleagues in managerial psychology and sociology. Furthermore, I think that Kantian moral theory provides a moral justification for some of the perspectives on human nature which are found in these disciplines. As I have argued elsewhere, standard economic theory either assumes that every person is a psychological egoist (utility maximizer) or ends up with the tautological assertion that people always do what is in their interest – an assertion that results from trying to build concern with others into the utility function.[17] This egoistic view of human nature is captured in Williamson's transaction cost economics when he assumes that managers must act as if people practice "opportunism with guile." Finally, it is captured in finance, among other disciplines, in what is called agency theory. A fundamental postulate of agency theory is that whenever the agent can act contrary to the interest of the principal (the person the agent serves) he or she will do so. If these assumptions were in fact universally true of human nature, ethics could never get started, since ethics maintains that in principle it is possible to act contrary to one's interest on grounds of morality. Given the divergence of these assumptions, it is no surprise that business ethics meets resistance in many schools of business.

However, there is no need for the amount of tension that exists. By giving up the assumption that economic exchange involves no transaction costs, a new subdiscipline of economics has been born and we have a better understanding of why certain activities occur in firms rather than in classical individual market exchanges. Some business scholars are dropping the assumption of perfect information to better understand exchanges under information asymmetry. Business ethicists ask business scholars to drop the utility maximizing assumption to better understand business exchanges under ethical constraints. Kant's moral philosophy provides a theory for doing that.

Ninth, to those who ask, "Why Kant?" I argue that Kant's moral framework provides a normative justification for a whole series of management practices that contemporaries term "enlightened." In what follows I give a Kantian justification for such practices as profit-sharing, employee participation, meaningful work, the collapse of hierarchies, and the move toward quality. What ties these practices together is not organizational theory, but rather ethical theory. These are the practices that a Kantian framework for evaluating the firm endorses. However, the reader should not think that Kantianism endorses everything on the plate of enlightened management. Some managers remain very paternalistic; they adopt rules that are for the employee's good even if the employee does not want them. Thus, they forbid employees to smoke, engage in dangerous recreational sports like skydiving, and they require that employees watch their weight; they may even provide health facilities in the plant as an encouragement to do so. Kantian moral philosophy rejects paternalism and thus it does not endorse every "enlightened" business practice. Beyond a certain reasonable working wage Kantian managers ought not to be overly concerned about the happiness of employees. To be so concerned the corporation would go far beyond what is required of it. It may even fall into paternalistic behavior, which a Kantian would find morally objectionable. Thus, I shall not be implementing Kant by showing how his theory justifies all the trendy enlightened management philosophies that are currently in fashion. Rather, I shall show how Kantianism gives a clear vision of what a business firm, if managed by a moral person, could become. Thus, in writing this book, I agree with Annette Baier that the applied philosopher needs to know something about the other discipline or disciplines in which he or she works. However, I do not think the contribution of philosophers need be as modest as she thinks.[18] Indeed, I hope this book contributes to scholarship in Kantian ethics by showing concretely how rich Kantian ethics can be. And I hope to contribute to management theory by showing that a business firm can be both moral and profitable. I believe Kant provides a mainstream non-Marxist criticism of the fundamental foundations of capitalism However, I also believe this criticism can be met as some work in organizational studies and human resources management has shown. This belief provides another main reason for writing this book.

Notes

1 It should be noted, as Richard DeGeorge has reminded me, that Kant thought all three formulations of the categorical imperative were equivalent. Thus, if an action violated one formulation, it violated the other two. In this book I make no attempt to defend Kant's equivalence thesis, although I believe that nothing I say is inconsistent with it.

2 However, Kirk Hart informs me that Kant was familiar with the work of Adam Smith. Christine Korsgaard has confirmed this fact, indicating that Kant was especially sympathetic to *The Theory of Moral Sentiments*.

3 Immanuel Kant, *Lectures on Ethics* 1775 (New York: Harper Torchbooks, 1963), pp. 160–1.

4 Barbara Herman, *The Practice of Moral Judgment* (Cambridge MA: Harvard University Press, 1993) p. 232.

5 Ibid., p. 206.

6 F. Crosby, *Relative Deprivation and Working Women* (New York: Oxford University Press, 1982).

7 B. Major and E. Konar, "An Investigation of Sex Differences in Pay Expectations and Their Possible Cause," *Academy of Management Journal* 27 (1984), pp. 777–92.

8 Jerald Greenberg, "Organizational Justice: Yesterday, Today, and Tomorrow," *Journal of Management* 16:2 (1990), p. 418.

9   Kant's theory has often been criticized on the grounds that it is utopian. See, for example, "Kant's Utopianism," chapter 4 in Thomas E. Hill Jr's *Dignity and Practical Reason in Kant's Moral Theory* (Ithaca, NY: Cornell University Press, 1992).

10 Robert C. Solomon, *Ethics and Excellence: Cooperation and Integrity in Business* (Oxford: Oxford University Press, 1992).

11 See, for example, Jonathan Dancy's "Ethical Particularism and Morally Relevant Properties," *Mind* XCII (1983), pp. 530–47 and his *Moral Reasons* (Oxford: Blackwell Publishers, 1993), as well as John McDowell, "Virtue and Reason," *Monist* 62 (1979), pp. 331–5; reworked as "Non-Cognitivism and Rule Following," in Steven Holtzmann and Christopher Leach (eds) *Wittgenstein: To Follow a Rule* (London: Routledge and Kegan Paul, 1981), pp. 141–62. Sarah Holtman has informed me that McDowell can be interpreted as making a stronger claim than the one made here. He may be interpreted as saying that moral principles cannot guide us.

12 For example, see Onora O'Neill, *Towards Justice and Virtue* (New York: Cambridge University Press, 1996), especially chapter 3.

13 See, for example, Michael Stocker's "The Schizophrenia of Modern Ethical Theories," *Journal of Philosophy* 73 (1976), pp. 453–66 and Bernard Williams's "Persons, Character and Morality" in *Moral Luck* (Cambridge and New York: Cambridge University Press, 1981), pp. 1–19.

14 The classic criticism in this regard is Lawrence Blum's *Friendship, Altruism, and Morality* (London and Boston: Routledge & Kegan Paul, 1980). Two defenders of Kant are Marcia Baron, "The Alleged Repugnance of Acting from the Motive of Duty," *Journal of Philosophy* 81 (1984), pp. 197–220, as well as *Kantian Ethics Almost Without Apology* (Ithaca, NY: Cornell University Press, 1996), and Jean Hampton, "Rethinking Reason," *American Philosophical Quarterly* 29 (1992), pp. 219–36.

15 For an excellent defense of Kant on this point see Barbara Herman, *The Practice of Moral Judgment*, chapter 9.

16 See Alexander Rosenberg, *Economics: Mathematical Politics or Science of Diminishing Returns* (Chicago: University of Chicago Press, 1992).

17 See my "Challenging the Egoistic Paradigm," *Business Ethics Quarterly* 1 (1991), pp. 1–21.

18 See Annette Baier, "Theory and Reflective Practices" and especially "Doing Without Moral Theory," both in *Postures of the Mind: Essays on Mind and Morals* (Minneapolis: University of Minnesota Press, 1985).

1

The Self-Defeating Nature of Immoral Business Practice

A close look reveals that a great deal of economic life depends for its viability on a certain limited degree of ethical commitment. Purely selfish behavior of individuals is really incompatible with any kind of settled economic life. There is almost invariably some element of trust and confidence. Much business is done on the basis of verbal assurance. (Kenneth J. Arrow)[1]

Introduction

Most business people in the United States would agree with the average American that a bedrock moral principle is the Golden Rule: "Do unto others as you will have them do unto you." The problem with the Golden Rule is that so long as you are willing to let others treat you in an immoral way, it seems as if you are allowed to treat them immorally as well. You sometimes find such an attitude in business expressed in the following way: I do not care if people try to deceive me or cheat me. That's how it is in business. The business world is a jungle. And since I am willing to let others try to deceive or cheat me, it is morally OK if I try to deceive or cheat them.

One business person and business academician even published a tamer version of that view in the *Harvard Business Review* about 30 years ago. Albert Carr had this to say about business:

We live in what is probably the most competitive of the world's civilized societies. Our customs encourage a high degree of aggression in the individual's striving for success. Business is our main area of competition and it has been ritualized into a game of strategy . . . That most businessmen are not indifferent to ethics in their private lives, everyone will agree. My point is that in their office lives they cease to be private citizens; they become game players who must be guided by a somewhat different set of standards. . . . The golden rule for all its value as an ideal for society is simply not feasible as a guide for business. A good part of the time the businessman is trying to do to others as he hopes others will not do unto him.[2]

And what does the game of business most resemble? For Carr it resembles the game of poker.

Poker's own brand of ethics is different from the ethical ideals of civilized human relationships. The game calls for distrust of the other fellow. It ignores the claim of friendship. Cunning deception and concealment of one's strength and intentions, not kindness and open heartedness, are vital in poker. No one thinks any worse of poker on that account. And no one should think any worse of the game of business because its standards of right and wrong differ from the prevailing traditions of morality in our society.[3]

Carr's article provoked a tremendous business response, much of it negative. Yet how could Carr be refuted? After all, many people who are not managers or corporate chief executive officers (CEOs) believe that business practice does not subscribe to the Golden Rule and that it does resemble the game of poker, but a poker game where some people have many more chips than others right from the beginning. One of the strengths of Kant's moral theory, I believe, is that it provides a definitive refutation of Carr. Kant's moral philosophy does nothing less than show that Carr's view is morally wrong because it is irrational. The task of this first chapter is to spell out Kant's argument and some of its implications.

Immoral Actions Are Based on Self-Defeating Maxims

To introduce Kant's point I begin, as Kant would not, by looking at some interesting facts. When on vacation in Ocean City, Maryland, my favorite seafood outlet had a large sign on the wall saying "We do not cash checks and here is why:" Below the sign and covering nearly the entire wall were photocopies of checks that had been returned and stamped in large letters "returned: insufficient funds." And while visiting Georgetown University in 1988, I saw that many of the merchants in Georgetown had a sign in their window saying "We do not cash Georgetown student checks." The obvious reason for those signs was that too many customers in that seafood shop and too many Georgetown students at that time were bouncing their checks.

There are also regional differences in the acceptability of checks and in the use of credit cards. Cashing checks on the east coast is very difficult and if the check is drawn on an out-of-town bank, cashing it is virtually impossible. However, in much of the Midwest the cashing of checks is common practice and in most stores in Minneapolis/St Paul, a metropolitan area of over two and a half million people, you can write a check for more than the amount of the purchase and get cash back!

Although more and more credit cards now carry photo identification, in the Midwest you can still use a credit card without such ID. In many places on the east coast if your credit card does not have a photo ID, you must present some other photo identification to use it. You also need a bank-issued photo ID to get cash from your own account at the bank where you do business. The convenience of a standard economic transaction is a function of the number of people who are honest and prompt in paying their bills. If enough people fail to adopt the maxim of honesty, economic transactions begin to break down and, of course, if bouncing checks and non-payment of bills were universal, the credit system would collapse.

And these examples are not limited to the United States. While lecturing on the implications of Kant's ethics for business ethics in Poland in 1995, I was informed that shortly after the fall of communism there was a bank collapse. The reason for the collapse? People did not repay their loans. Finally, experts almost universally agree that one of the major impediments to the development of capitalism in Russia is the failure to pay one's bills. A supplier is reluctant to provide a product if it does not get paid. What I intend to show is that this is what a Kantian would expect and indeed could even predict.

Inconsistency and Immorality

To illustrate Kant's strategy consider his example of making a promise with no intention of keeping it. Would such an action be morally wrong? To answer that question Kant would instruct you to construct a general principle (maxim) that captured the action. In this specific case the principle (maxim) would be "It is morally permissible to make a promise with the intention of breaking it." Kant then instructs us to ask whether such a maxim could become a universal law. The answer is "no" because that maxim is contradictory. It is contradictory because if everyone could break promises, promises would never get made. If such a maxim were universalized the very notion of promises would make no sense. As Kant says:

> And could I say to myself that everyone may make a false promise when he is in a difficulty from which he cannot escape? Immediately I see that I could will the lie but not a universal law to lie. For with such a law there would be no promises at all, inasmuch as it would be futile to make a pretense of my intention in regard to future actions to those who would not believe this pretense or – if they over hastily did so – would pay me back in my own coin. Thus my maxim would necessarily destroy itself as soon as it was made a universal law.[4]

The general point to be made from Kant's discussion of the immorality of lying is that self-contradictory universalized maxims are morally prohibited. That is why it is wrong to break a promise: the maxim for that action could not be consistently universalized.

Kant's central insight is captured in the first formulation of his categorical imperative. The first and most often quoted formulation of the categorical imperative says "Act only on that maxim by which you can at the same time will that it should become a universal law."[5] Some preliminary explanation is immediately required. Kant wants to show that some principles (maxims) upon which actions are based are inconsistent or self-defeating. It is impossible for everyone to act on the basis of the principle; that is why the principle could not be accepted as a universal law. If an individual acted on a principle that it would be impossible for

#4 - Kant - instruct you to construct a general
principle a maxim that captured the action

+ First formulation of the categorical imperative

"Act only on the maxim by which you can
at the same time will that it should become
a law" —

A deceit full promise.

everyone to follow, that individual's action would be wrong. That is precisely what was wrong with the idea of making a promise with the intention of breaking it.

Despite the fact that many people are likely to be sympathetic to the criticism of Kant made by John Stuart Mill, Kant wants to remove consequences from the consideration of what makes an act right or wrong. Mill argues that Kant utterly fails to do so. Mill thinks Kant answers the question "Why is a deceitful promise wrong?" by saying that the universalization of deceitful promises leads to bad consequences. And so it does. But that is not the reason why a deceitful promise is bad. A deceitful promise is bad because the maxim which would allow the universalization of deceitful promises is self-contradictory. Kant is very clear about that.

Thus, the categorical imperative functions as a test to see if the principle (maxim) upon which an action is based is morally permissible. So long as the principle for one's action passes the test of the categorical imperative, then the action may be undertaken. A business manager who accepts Kantian morality would ask, for any given decision, whether the principle on which the decision is based passes the test of the categorical imperative. If it does, then the decision would be morally permissible. With respect to the first formulation of the categorical imperative, the business manager would ask whether the maxim which describes the proposed action could be willed universally without contradiction. If the maxim could be so willed, then the contemplated action is morally permissible. If it could not be so willed, then it is morally forbidden.

Applications to Business

Now the making of promises is a practice. It is important to note with Christine Korsgaard that the self-contradiction interpretation of the first formulation of the categorical imperative works well for the violation of the rules of a practice: "a practice has a standard purpose and if its rules are universally violated it ceases to be efficacious for this person, and so ceases to exist."[6] Since business consists, at least in part, of a number of practices with standard purposes we might expect Kant's universal law formulation of the categorical imperative to work well in business and so it does.

Consider the breaking of contracts, an issue widely discussed in contemporary business.[7] A contract is an agreement between two or more parties, usually enforceable by law, for the doing or not doing of some specific thing. A contract is one of the more formal ways of making a promise. The hiring of employees, the use of credit, the ordering and supplying of goods, and the notion of warranty, to name but a few, all make use of contracts. If a maxim that permitted contract breaking were universalized, there could be no contracts (contracts would cease to exist.) No one would enter into a contract if he or she believed the other party had no intention of honoring it. A universalized maxim that permitted contract breaking would be self-defeating.

Consider theft. Theft by employees, managers, and customers is a major problem in business. Is stealing wrong? Suppose that an employee, angry at her boss for some reason, considered stealing something from the firm. Could a maxim which permitted stealing be universalized? It could not. In order to steal, there must be an institution of private property. Why? Consider the alternatives. If there were no scarcity so that all goods and services were readily available for the taking, then there would be no concept of stealing. Similarly, if all goods and services belonged to everyone. The concept of stealing does not apply in worlds where there is no scarcity or where everything belongs to everyone. (Of course, if someone took something that belonged to everyone and tried to keep it for himself, then you might call that stealing. However, that would be because the person tried to take something that belonged to everyone and make it his private property.) Obviously, neither of those worlds is our world and the institution of private property has been devised to deal with the fact that goods and services are in limited supply and that universal collective ownership is impractical. If a maxim that permitted stealing were universalized, there could be no such thing as private property. If everyone was free to take from everyone else, then nothing could be owned. Given the practical necessity of some form of private property, a universalized maxim that permitted stealing would be self-defeating. Thus, if the employee steals from her boss, what she does is morally wrong.

Now consider an objection to Kant's no-self-contradiction requirement raised by Hegel, Bradley, and several others. Simply put the argument runs like this: If there is a practice of private property, then a maxim that permitted stealing would be self-contradictory. But there is nothing self-contradictory about a world without the practice of private property. So Kant's argument fails.

But as Korsgaard has argued, this criticism misses Kant's point.[8] Kant is simply arguing that if there is a practice of private property then a maxim which permitted stealing would be logically self-contradictory. In all capitalist societies, and indeed in most societies generally, we do have private property and so a maxim that permitted stealing in societies with private property would be self-contradictory.

We can see this when we consider an example that does not have the ideological baggage that accompanies a term like "private property." Take the practice of lining (queuing) up. There is nothing inconsistent about a society that does not have such a practice. However, in a society which does have the practice, cutting into line is morally wrong. The maxim on which the act of line-cutting is based cannot be made a universal law. An attempt to universalize line-cutting destroys the very notion of a line.

What is helpful about Korsgaard's response on behalf of Kant against Hegel and his other critics, is that it allows the categorical imperative to work for the rules of any institution or practice. Indeed, the test of the categorical imperative becomes a principle of fair play. One of the essential features of fair play is that one should not make an exception of oneself. For example, Kant says,

> When we observe ourselves in any transgression of a duty, we find that we do not actually will that our maxim should become a universal law. That is impossible for us; rather the contrary of this maxim should remain as the law generally, and we only take the liberty of making an exception to it for ourselves or for the sake of our inclination, and for this one occasion. Consequently, if we weighed everything from one and the same standpoint, namely reason, we would come upon a contradiction in our own will, viz., that a certain principle is objectively necessary as a universal law and yet subjectively does not hold universally but rather admits exceptions.[9]

We now can use Kant's first formulation of the categorical imperative to show that whenever someone, including someone in business, agrees to follow the rules for cooperative behavior and then violates those rules for personal gain, such a violation is morally wrong. A maxim that permitted universal violation of the rules is self-defeating. A universally violated rule is not a rule.

This kind of analysis shows that free-loading is morally wrong. A free-loader is one who accepts the advantages of the rules for cooperative behavior, but then either violates the rules or fails to contribute her share in supporting them. Must of us would characterize free-loading as unfair or unjust. Kant's universalizability formulation of the categorical imperative explains why it is unjust. If free-loading were universalized, then the rules that made cooperative activity possible could not exist.

This Kantian insight has been accepted by John Rawls. Rawls asks us to consider an individual who voluntarily participates in a social institution and thereby accepts its rules and regulations. Presumably these rules work out to the long-run benefit of the participants in the institution or are very likely to do so, otherwise the person would not voluntarily participate in the institution. However, one who accepts the benefits of an institution, including the benefits derived when others participating in the institution follow the rules and regulations, but who himself does not play by the rules, is unfair. He is a free-loader: one who accepts the benefits without paying any of the costs.

> In everyday life an individual, if he is so inclined, can sometimes win even greater benefits for himself by taking advantage of the cooperative efforts of others. Sufficiently many persons may be doing so that when special circumstances allow him not to contribute (perhaps his omissions will not be found out), he gets the best of both worlds.[10]

What's wrong with free-loading? You are not making a contribution to the institution that relies on the contributions of those participating in the institution – a contribution which you agreed to make when you agreed to participate in the institution. That is what it means to be a free-loader. But of course if a maxim permitting free-loading were universalized, the institution itself would be undermined.

These Kantian-type arguments apply to almost all competitive situations as well. Capitalism is a system of economic competition, but even competitive activity requires rules regulating competition.

As Adam Smith and all after him have realized, capitalism requires rules protecting property rights, enforcing contracts, and settling disputes; otherwise business activity would be impossible. As indicated at the outset some business people describe the business world as a jungle, but if it truly were a jungle, business itself would not survive.

Someone who enters a competitive activity and violates the rules regulating that competition acts immorally. Why? Because if the rules regulating competition were universally violated, those "rules" would no longer be rules. If regulatory rules are universally violated, regulation is impossible. Such activity would be self-defeating in two senses. Universal violation of the rule would make the rule nugatory. And since the rule is one that is required to keep competition from degenerating into chaos or a war of all against all, the universalized violation of rules would make welfare-enhancing competition itself self-defeating.

It Seems Right in Theory But Does It Work in Practice?

I have frequently used these arguments with executives who may find them theoretically persuasive, but who, nonetheless, think their practical implication is limited. They point out that in the real world in which business actually operates not everyone breaks contracts and not everyone free-loads. Some do but not all. Knowing that, isn't it to the strategic advantage of the firm to be the one who does break contracts or otherwise free-loads? After all, in terms of pure self-interest, the best world for a person or firm is one where everyone else plays by the rules except you, isn't it?

In asking that question I point out that one is no longer asking a question of ethics (the executives are already convinced that theoretically such activity is wrong), but rather a prudential question of strategy. Although Kant would feel no need to answer it, Kantian-type arguments can be brought to bear on the prudential question. The common approach of these arguments is to show that the self-defeating nature of actions based on maxims that cannot be universalized cut in long before complete universalization would take place. That was the point with my Georgetown student example.

The fact that Georgetown students bounced more checks than the rest of the population did not bring about the collapse of payment by check. But it did for Georgetown students who did business in the proximity of Georgetown University.

What is significant but often overlooked by philosophers is that Kant's universalizability formulation of the categorical imperative is subject to empirical support. In some ways that should not be surprising. If someone tries to create a round square we can predict that no one will succeed. Similarly, if stealing or cheating when universalized is conceptually incoherent, then we would expect the collapse of certain institutions and practices if stealing or cheating became universal in our society, or at the very least those institutions would not be available for a subset of society. Now we do not have a case of universalized cheating any more than we have a case of absolute zero or a perfect vacuum. But we do have close approximations. We can empirically observe that Kantian-type effects take place when actions whose maxims cannot be universalized reach a certain threshold. We began the chapter by providing examples of what happens to credit when people do not pay their bills. A Kantian could predict that if enough checks of seafood customers bounce, the seafood store will stop taking checks. She could also predict that if people do not repay loans, the banks will fail.

There are positive stories that illustrate Kant's point as well. That is, there are stories showing that when a threshold of morality is reached, certain institutions become possible and, when economically feasible, will develop. Russia is in the process of starting a stock exchange. The difficulties in doing so, however, have been great, in part because company spokespersons would not provide accurate financial information about their companies. As a Kantian would expect, investors will not be forthcoming if they believe that the members of the exchange lie about their companies. Gradually, a few companies including Irkutsk Energo, Bratsky LPK, and Rostelecom were able to establish a reputation as truthtellers. These companies were then able to attract investors and have done well. The *Wall Street Journal* put it this way:

> When the chief engineer of Irkutsk Energo addressed a gathering of 250 Western fund managers last March, he gave a straightforward presentation of the Russian utility's assets, liabilities and investment

policy. This was anything but typical in Russia where enterprises usually withhold even basic information from investors. . . . This winter (1995) a few mavericks proved the value of corporate glasnost. As these companies drew foreign interest, others followed. Of the 50 most actively traded Russian companies, 10 are ardently wooing foreign investors. Last year there were two. . . . "There is a clear differentiation in the market between those companies that get it and those that don't," says Nancy Curtin head of the Emerging Europe funds for Baring Asset Management.[11]

In trying to establish a stock market, the Russians faced the problem that lying about the finances of the firm was perceived to be nearly universal. As a Kantian would expect, so long as the perception was held Russian society could not have a stock market that reflected the rational values of the firms. Since investors knew that the information about the firms was false, there was no alternative way for them to get a reasonable figure about a firm's value. (Thus, the Securities and Exchange Commission provides a genuine contribution in the USA because it forces firms to be more truthful.) However, once a sufficient number of firms were perceived as being truthful about their finances, the stock prices of those firms rose rapidly to reflect rational expectations of the firms' worth.

And the success of these honest firms has led other firms to be more honest, to the point where the Russian stock market is thriving. The March 24, 1997 *Business Week* carried a story entitled "The Rush to Russia." In 1996 the Russian stock market was up 127 percent and it had already gained 65 percent in 1997. Of course, more honesty on the part of Russian companies is not the explanation for the rise in the stock market. Rather, sufficient honesty is a necessary condition for there to be a stock market at all.

As an aside, business ethicists are often asked how a business that wishes to be ethical should behave when other businesses are clearly behaving unethically. These executives would like to be ethical but believe they would be at a competitive disadvantage if they were ethical. And sometimes they would be. But, as our example of the Russian stock market shows, sometimes a firm has a clear competitive advantage if it is ethical when most other firms are not. Nearly all of us have horror stories to tell about auto-repair shops. Suffice it to say that the industry does not have a good reputation. Think of how successful an auto-repair shop would be if it had a reputation for honesty. This point is not merely theoretical. In Bloomington Minnesota I dealt with a devout Christian who left the repair facility of a major dealer to open his own repair facility. I was one of his first customers. I could call in the morning and get my car fixed that day. Within a year, I might have to wait nearly a week because he was so busy. In relating these positive examples, I am not arguing that one ought to be honest because it pays. I am pointing out that sometimes as a matter of fact it does. More remarkably in some cases it pays the most when most other competitors are not honest. Sometimes, contrary to popular opinion, the best competitive position for you is when all (or a large number of) your competitors are perceived to be (or are) dishonest and you are and are perceived to be honest. My car repairman in Minnesota occupies just that world.

The force of failure to follow the categorical imperative can be found in business practices themselves. Both the strategy literature and the popular business press extol the virtues of strategic alliances. In an era where companies are urged to focus on their core competencies (those things which they do most effectively), strategic alliances have become a crucial part of doing business. The Kantian moral philosopher would urge her firm to avoid alliances with firms that are not moral in Kant's sense, i.e., they constantly practice business according to maxims that are not universalizable, e.g., they lie or cheat. Why would a firm want to partner with another firm that lies and cheats, especially when all members of a partnership are joint and severally liable for the product they jointly produce?

Supplier problems are not unique to the economies emerging from communism. Failure to heed Kant's dictum that a self-contradictory maxim cannot be universalized has created tremendous problems for General Motors and Volkswagen. General Motors promoted Jose Ignacio Lopez de Arroirtua (Lopez) on the basis of his success in lowering the cost of supplier products. His success in this area arose primarily through his practice of continually reopening negotiations with suppliers and providing the proprietary information of one supplier to other suppliers so that these suppliers could provide the product more cheaply. A morally sensitive person would characterize these activities as lying and stealing respectively. As we have shown, the maxims that permit lying and stealing cannot be universalized. Thus, what Lopez did was wrong.

And General Motors made an imprudent decision in promoting

him. Is it any surprise that Lopez left GM for the German company Volkswagen, allegedly taking with him several associates and many cartons of GM's proprietary purchasing data? Furthermore, is it any surprise that, in a recent survey, the suppliers of auto parts rated GM worst of all the automakers? How will GM fare as it enters what *Fortune* calls the new economy where cars cost less because the auto industry relies more on cheaper high-quality suppliers?[12] The strategic advice is that manufacturers should partner with their suppliers. But why would a supplier want to partner with a manufacturer that has promoted someone who lied and stole from them?

To strengthen this point, the November 25, 1996 issue of *Business Week* indicates that Lopez's former dealings with suppliers of GM have brought similar problems to Volkswagen. Lopez is expected to be charged by German prosecutors with the theft of trade secrets. Meanwhile in the USA, GM began legal action against Volkswagen CEO Ferdinand Piech and other company executives for up to $4 billion in damages.[13] On November 29, 1996 the Volkswagen Board accepted Lopez's "resignation." Shortly thereafter GM and Volkswagen reached a settlement, but Lopez's problems in both the USA and Germany remain.

In arguing that sound ethical business practices can support a positive bottom line, I am not arguing that this is always the case. Sometimes ethics does not pay but costs. In those cases Kantian morality requires that a business firm do what is ethically required even if it does not pay. However, I hope I have shown that doing what is morally required is not always unprofitable. Sometimes being moral enhances the bottom line rather than reduces it.

In summary, I have tried to show how Kant's universalizability formulation of the categorical imperative can be used to test the moral legitimacy of contemplated actions in business. In using that test we have an argument as to why certain actions like the breaking of contracts, stealing, and competing unfairly are morally wrong. We have also seen that if such immoral actions such as those cited cross a critical threshold, the business institutions that presuppose norms of truthfulness and fairness will become unstable and in extreme circumstances even cease to exist. Furthermore, through the use of numerous examples I have tried to show that Kant's arguments are of more than theoretical interest. They have predictable real-world applications.

Objections to the Application of Kantian Ethics to Business

Many commentators, especially those critical of Kant, have argued that Kant is an absolutist in ethics; that for Kant, being ethical is a matter of following a set of absolute moral rules that has no room for exceptions. On that view Kantian business ethics would consist of a set of absolute rules that business should follow without exception. But the view that Kantian moral philosophy is a set of absolute rules is a distortion of Kant.

The categorical imperative is absolute in the sense that if the principle (maxim) for an action is not in conformity with it, then that action is wrong, no if's or but's: that is what it *means* to say that an imperative is categorical. A hypothetical imperative, in contrast to a categorical imperative, is an if-then imperative. "If you want a good job, you ought to go to college" is a hypothetical imperative. Thus, one need only obey hypothetical imperatives if one values the ends. However, categorical imperatives are obligatory on their face. Certainly, in some respects Kantian ethics is stringent. Principles for actions that fail the test of the categorical imperative are wrong.

As we shall see in later chapters, Kant believed he had three versions of one absolute moral rule – the categorical imperative. One lives a moral life if the maxims upon which one acts pass the tests of the categorical imperative (and if a maxim violates the categorical imperative, one abstains from the action out of duty or, alternatively, where an action is required by the categorical imperative one does the action out of duty). Acting out of respect for the categorical imperative is the central message of Kantian ethics.

Having said that, a categorical imperative still provides flexibility in ethics. If the only alternative is between a principle that fails the test and a principle that is the logical contradictory of the principle that fails the test, then the logical contradictory of the principle that fails the test is morally required. But there is often a number of alternatives to the principle that is forbidden by the test of the categorical imperative. If a person has a number of alternatives and the principles on which each alternative is based pass the test of the categorical imperative, then the person is morally free to choose whatever alternative she likes. To illustrate this point, in chapters 2 and 3 I shall argue that Kantian moral theory requires that employees in a corporation have a right to participate in formulating the rules and policies that affect them. However, I will give several examples of different participative schemes all of which would meet the requirement for participation and thus pass the tests of the categorical imperative.

Extending the Reach of Categorical Imperatives: Pragmatically Inconsistent Maxims

So far our discussion has assumed that the proper way to interpret the universalizability formulation of the categorical imperative is that if the maxim for an action is self-contradictory, then the action would be morally wrong. However, contemporary scholars, and apparently even Kant himself, recognize that self-contradiction is not sufficient to do all the work that Kant wants the categorical imperative to do. One can see this when one notices that at least two, if not all, of the examples of prohibited actions in the *Foundations of the Metaphysics of Morals* are not based on maxims that are self-contradictory. In that work Kant argues that the categorical imperative requires that, in addition to not lying, we develop our talents, we not commit suicide, and that we have a duty of beneficence to help others. But what is self-contradictory about a maxim that states that one is not under an obligation to help others or a maxim which states that one need not develop one's talents?

To deal with these cases, I note that nearly all commentators agree that Kant himself recognized at least two senses, if not kinds, of self-contradiction. Kant says,

> We must be able to will that a maxim of our action become a universal law; this is the canon of the moral estimation of our action generally. Some actions are of such a nature that their maxim cannot even be *thought* as a universal law of nature without contradiction, far from it being possible that one could will that it should be such. In others this internal impossibility is not found, though it is still impossible to *will* that the maxim should be raised to the universality of a law of nature, because such a will would contradict itself.[14]

According to Christine Korsgaard we can distinguish between logical (conceptual) contradiction and pragmatic contradiction. On the logical interpretation a self-contradictory universalized maxim is one that proposes an inconceivable action or policy. On the pragmatic interpretation a contradictory maxim is one that promotes an action that would be inconsistent with your purpose if everyone tried to act on it.[15] The notion of pragmatic contradiction can be explained by using three of Kant's examples: the already familiar lying promise and the failure to develop our talents and to come to the aid of others. Korsgaard applies the pragmatic interpretation to two of these examples as follows:

> If a thwarted purpose is a practical contradiction, we must understand the contradiction in the will test in this way: we must find some purpose or purposes which belong essentially to the will, and in the world where maxims that fail these tests are universal law, these essential purposes will be thwarted, because the means of achieving them will be unavailable. Examples of purposes that might be thought to be essential to the will are its general effectiveness in the pursuit of its ends, and its freedom to adopt and pursue new ends. The arguments for self-development and mutual aid will then be that without the development of human talents and powers and the resources of mutual cooperation, the will's effectiveness and freedom will be thwarted.[16]

Although Korsgaard believes that all of Kant's examples are amenable to a pragmatic-contradiction interpretation, in the *Foundations* passage quoted above Kant goes on to use the two interpretations of self-contradiction to imply that violations of our perfect duties, e.g., not to lie, involve conceptual contradictions, whereas violations of our imperfect duties, e.g., our duty of beneficence, are pragmatic (or volitional, as O'Neill calls them) contradictions. As a matter of clarification, perfect duties are duties we are always bound to fulfill, whereas imperfect duties are duties that we need to fulfill on some occasions but not on all occasions.[17] Thus, we must never lie, but we need not always act with beneficence to others. Thus, the contradiction involved in violations of perfect duties involves a conceptual contradiction. A universalized deceitful promise is a conceptual absurdity. However, a universalized maxim not to develop one's talents involves a contradiction in one's will. Thus, violations of maxims for imperfect duties involve not a contradiction in the maxim but a contradiction in the will of the one who holds the maxim.[18]

By this point I am sure the reader is asking "What is the significance of all this for business ethics?" In what follows I shall show how certain business practices, although not conceptual absurdities, are volitional absurdities or pragmatic contradictions and thus are morally wrong. For example, any business practice that undermines trust will result in a pragmatic contradiction. If a business person says that she will not trust anyone in any business transaction, she seems not to be contradicting herself. However, I hope to show that she would be involved in what Korsgaard has called a pragmatic contradiction. To avoid a pragmatic contradiction, one should not act on a maxim that, if universalized, would defeat the purpose behind the maxim. Korsgaard explains a pragmatic contradiction as follows:

> The test is carried out by imagining, in effect, that the action you propose to perform in carrying out your purpose is the standard procedure for carrying out that purpose. What the test shows to be forbidden are just those actions whose efficacy in achieving their purposes depends upon their being exceptional. . . . For instance, in the false promising case, the difficulty is that the man's end – getting the money – cannot be achieved by his means – making a false promise – in the world of the universalized maxim. The efficacy of the false promise as a means of securing money depends on the fact that not everyone uses promises that way.[19]

Before arguing that failure to trust or be trustworthy in business involves a pragmatic contradiction, I wish to start with a business example that has been discussed by Kantian ethicists. Onora O'Neill has argued that competition, construed in a certain way, does involve a pragmatic (volitional) contradiction.

Does business competition involve a pragmatic contradiction?

Let us begin with Onora O'Neill's example of competitive games. She argues that there is no pragmatic inconsistency in deciding to participate in competitive games per se, but there is a pragmatic inconsistency in deciding to participate with the intention of winning. Her one-sentence argument for this claim is that such an intention would make an exception of oneself.[20] Presumably she thinks one is making an exception of oneself by wanting to win and wanting no one else to win.

But I think O'Neill is mistaken here. A person can certainly will that every participant in a competitive game can enter with the intention of winning. In fact in competitive sports that is exactly the intention that everyone has. No one is making an exception of herself by *intending* to win even when everyone knows not everyone *can* win. The maxim "I will try to win" does not involve a pragmatic contradiction. The maxim "I will win" of course does involve a pragmatic inconsistency since everyone in a competitive game cannot be a winner. But rather trying to win, which certainly everyone can and indeed does try to do, seems legitimate because that maxim is consistent with the categorical imperative. The other way to be involved in a contradiction in competitive sports is to not follow the rules, i.e., to cheat. As we have seen, cheating involves a conceptual inconsistency and on Korsgaard's view a pragmatic inconsistency as well.

O'Neill's other example involves economic competition. Her argument depends on our acceptance of principles of rational intending, especially the fifth principle called "The Principle of Intending the Further Results." This principle says that "it is a requirement of rationality that the foreseeable results of the specific intentions adopted in acting on a given underlying intention be consistent with the underlying intention."[21] At this point, it is best to let O'Neill speak for herself:

> I can adopt the underlying intention of improving my economic well-being, and the specific intention of doing so by competing effectively with others. The maxim of my action can be consistently universalized. There is no conceptual contradiction in intending everyone's economic condition to improve. . . . But if an agent intends his or her economic advance to be achieved solely by competitive strategies, this nexus of intentions cannot consistently be willed as universal law, because the further results of universal competitive activity, by itself, are inconsistent with universal economic advance. If everyone seeks to advance by these (and no other) methods, the result will not put everyone ahead economically. A maxim of economic progress combined with the specific intention of achieving

progress merely by competitive strategies cannot be universalized, any more than the intention of looking over the heads of a crowd can universally be achieved by everyone in the crowd standing on tiptoes. . . . Competitive means are inherently effective only for some. Competition must have losers as well as winners. . . . Once we consider what it would be to intend the consequences of universal competition – the usually unintended consequences – we can see that there is an inconsistency not between universal competitive activity and universal economic progress, but between the *further results of intending only universal competitive activity and universal economic progress.*[22]

Whether this argument is correct or not depends on a number of complicated issues. First, economists would argue that under perfect competition in market activity there is universal economic progress, in the sense that there is no additional state of affairs where everyone is better off without anyone being worse off. In other words pure competition is Pareto optimal.

However, the universal economic progress is a collective achievement compatible with wide inequalities within society. Is there anything inconsistent about people willing to participate in economic activity with the risk that they be one of those who loses and loses a great deal? Although O'Neill has not made that argument, she could argue that the requirement that we develop our talents rationally requires that we not enter an activity that might produce losses so severe that we would not have the means to develop our talents.

Defenders of the competitive market could also argue along the lines of public finance theory. If part of the understanding of competitive economic activity is that the government will protect the severe losers by providing a welfare floor paid for by transfer payments by the winners, then either there is no pragmatic inconsistency because government provision of a welfare floor is part of the competitive system, or government corrects for the pragmatic inconsistency by providing a welfare floor. It may be that such a concession proves O'Neill's point. You cannot will both universal competitive activity and universal economic progress for all individuals. In a moral society we cannot let the market be the sole determinant of economic welfare.

I wish to take O'Neill's insight in a slightly different direction. I take the significance of O'Neill's analysis to be that she has provided a Kantian argument for claiming that the market must either consist of more than purely competitive behavior or that a market that is purely competitive must be corrected by another institution such as government.

I think we can show that the market must consist of more than purely competitive behavior. Totally unconstrained competition that does not forbid the use of force or fraud is ultimately self-defeating. If more and more people break the rules, structured rule-bound competition degenerates into the law of the jungle. Obviously that has bad consequences for business, but that is a consequentialist point. More importantly, if you are in a jungle-like situation, rule-governed competitive activity is self-defeating and thus is pragmatically contradictory.

Contrary to some of the rhetoric, the world of business is not simply a matter of competition, even of regulated competition. Successful business activity depends as much on cooperative behavior as it does on competitive behavior. A task of management theory is to show how the competitive strands and the cooperative strands of business are weaved together to make a successful whole. I wish to conclude this chapter by showing that on the pragmatic interpretation of the first formulation of the categorical imperative, persons in a business relationship must be both trustworthy and trusting.

Why Neither Being Trustworthy nor Not Trusting in Business Involves a Pragmatic Contradiction

Management theorists have discovered trust. At the 1996 annual meeting of the Academy of Management, I believe there were more papers on this topic than on any other. – and most of those papers were not in sessions sponsored by the Social Issues in Management Division (where most business ethicists reside), but rather in main-stream sessions on strategy and organizational behavior. Trust has become significant because it is seen as an important ingredient for competitive success. Management theory seems to be endorsing the following hypothetical imperative:

If one wants to achieve one's business purposes (profitability), then one must establish trust with one's various corporate stakeholders.

We need to do considerable work to transform this prudential argument for trust into an ethical obligation required by the categorical imperative. Can the argument from management theory be cast in a new light so that trust is required of business by the first formulation of the categorical imperative? What will need to be shown is that business practice requires trust, so that one who acts in ways that violate trust or make trust on the part of others impossible is pragmatically (volitionally) inconsistent. With respect to showing this inconsistency Korsgaard is instructive once again:

> We must find some purpose or purposes which belong essentially to the will, and in the world where maxims that fail these tests are universal law, these essential purposes will be thwarted, because the means of achieving them will be unavailable.[23]

I think Korsgaard's insights here can be helpful as we transform the prudential argument for trust into a categorical argument. Eventually, I shall argue that trust is essential in most business relationships if business is to achieve its ends. But first the prudential end of profit-making must be seen as an ethical obligation. The first step is to claim that

1   A manager has a contractual obligation to manage the firm in the best interests of the corporation.
     To this normative obligation you add the factual claim
2   A manager can manage the firm in the best interests of the corporation only if she builds trust among the corporate stakeholders.
     From the normative claim combined with the factual claim you can conclude that
3   A manager has an obligation to build trust among the corporate stakeholders.

Since the manager has made a promise (has a contractual obligation) to manage in the best interest of the corporation, and since building trusting relationships among the corporate stakeholders is necessary to fulfill that promise, then a manager has a moral obligation and not merely a prudential one for building those trusting relationships. The normative claim is widely accepted, although what counts as the interests of the corporation varies as to whether one holds to a traditional stockholder finance model of the firm or to a more contemporary stakeholder theory. More will be said about the content of this obligation from a Kantian perspective as the book progresses. However, I take it for granted that nearly everyone accepts the normative premise.

There is more skepticism about the factual premise. One thing the business ethicist needs to do is provide evidence from the management literature that the factual premise is true. We need to show that trust is essential to business practice, so essential that a maxim which undermines trust can be shown to be pragmatically (volitionally) self-defeating. Following Korsgaard, I seek to show that actions that violate trust are inconsistent with the essential purposes of business. In other words, in the absence of trust, business as we know it would be impossible.

Kenneth Boulding made this point when he said that "without an integrative framework, exchange itself cannot develop, because exchange, even in its most primitive form, involves trust and credibility."[24] We can illustrate Boulding's point by looking at a simple case of cash-for-product transfer. In almost all such cases, either the purchaser receives the goods before paying for them, or the purchaser pays before receiving the goods. Seldom is the transfer simultaneous. If trust does not exist on both sides, the transfer of cash for product will not take place, a not uncommon occurrence in Russia as previously pointed out. Thus, trust is essential for even the most basic business transaction to take place.[25]

Let us now move from a simple cash-for-product transfer to more complicated business transactions. This line of argument that maintains trust is essential for business has been made by Francis Fukuyama in his book *Trust*. He says:

> It is perhaps easier to appreciate the economic value of trust if we consider what a world devoid of trust would look like. If we had to approach every contract with the assumption that our partners would try to cheat us if they could, then we would have to spend a considerable amount of time bulletproofing the document to make

sure that there were no legal loopholes by which we could be taken advantage of. Contracts would be endlessly long, spelling out every possible contingency and defining every conceivable obligation.[26]

Fukuyama is discussing the transaction costs of doing business and pointing out that in the absence of trust, the transaction costs would become so high that commercial transactions as we know them would become prohibitively expensive. The necessity of having lawyers develop contracts that cover all contingencies makes the cost of business impossibly expensive.[27] Again, there is empirical evidence that helps establish the Kantian point. As the trust between doctors and patients broke down, patients sued their doctors more frequently. This caused malpractice insurance premiums to rise. In fact they rose so high in certain specialties that some people practicing those specialties were forced to give them up. At some point the specialty would cease to exist.

Yet another example is found in government procurement. The lack of trust that exists between government and private contractors is enormous. Fukuyama hypothesizes that this lack of trust can explain the $800 toilet seats the government purchased.[28] Here is the argument. Since many weapons systems are one-of-a-kind products, there are few suppliers. Thus, prices are not driven by the market but are negotiated on a cost-plus basis. An alternative would be to have government officials use their discretion. However, since it is assumed that contractors are out to cheat the taxpayers and that officials are likely to abuse their freedom, lengthy detailed specifications are drawn up with numerous auditors hired by both parties to insure compliance. The result is $800 toilet seats.[29] Generalize to all of business practice and the transaction costs resulting from lack of trust become prohibitive.

And this argument is not simply consequentialist. What I am trying to present is a Kantian argument to the effect that a market rests to some extent on trust. As there is less and less trust, you reach a point where the necessity to use lawyers to write detailed contracts imposes transaction costs such that the economic transactions do not resemble a market at all. Government purchasing for the military is quite far removed from the market paradigm of consumers buying vegetables in the supermarket. In a genuine market at current prices a toilet seat would not cost $800.

Another way to argue this point is to show that trust can provide a competitive advantage. Now it is essential for the survival of the firm, and thus in the best interests of the firm, that it exploit competitive advantages. Two colleagues, Philip Bromiley and Larry Cummings, have developed a set of seven hypotheses which link trust to competitive advantage.[30] Bromiley and Cummings define trust as keeping one's word and not taking undue advantage (behaving opportunistically) when one has the capability of doing so. By commenting on some of these hypotheses, the reader can see how trust can provide a competitive advantage.

In a trusting relationship we believe that those we trust will not take undue advantage of opportunistic situations. Given that belief, we will control and monitor those we trust less than those we do not. And in so doing we will save transaction costs. It costs more to deal with those we do not trust than to deal with those we do. As a firm considers strategic alliances, one of the most important characteristics that a potential partner should have is that it be trustworthy. No firm can afford to be exploited because another firm takes advantage or fails to live up to their end of the bargain.

A Bromiley and Cummings hypothesis deals with the kinds of monitoring and control used in a trusting as compared to a nontrusting relationship – an issue of particular concern to those engaged in human resources management. According to Bromiley and Cummings, higher levels of trust should result in:

1   increased use of multiple and nonfinancial criteria for measuring performance and less use of detailed process controls and financial outcome measurement;

2   lower frequency of evaluation, and evaluation with a "mentoring" direction rather than an "evaluation and reward orientation";

3   lower requirements for detailed process information in both operational and project planning and monitoring.[31]

The essential point here, I believe, is that trusting relationships change the nature of monitoring in a way that provides a competitive advantage. In nontrusting relationships the supervisor functions as a policeman. In a trusting relationship the supervisor functions as a mentor, the way a professor functions with a doctoral student.

Such a mentoring relationship permits the use of qualitative data and it reduces the amount of quantitative data, the frequency of evaluation, and the amount of detail. All of this saves time and money.

Moreover, of late there has been much discussion of the necessity of teamwork in order to survive. Workers need to be "empowered," that is they are to be given more responsibility and discretion in their work. If teamwork and empowerment are not to be empty rhetoric then the nature of supervision must be more of a mentoring type than a policing type. Greater trust will be a key element in any cost savings that result from eliminating layers of management and the empowerment of employee teams. I will have much more to say about these issues in chapters 2 and 3.

Some of Bromiley and Cummings's work indicates that trust might be required to make some profitable interactions possible *within* firms as well as *between* firms. For example, American manufacturing enterprises have traditionally suffered from two disadvantages. First, the engineering team that designs a product does its work separately. Those who manufacture the product have little if anything to say about its design. As a result problems with a prototype do not appear until the manufacturing stage. Much time is lost as the prototype is redesigned to meet the requirements of mass production.

Second, the sales force has incentives to sell as much product as it can; the commission system is what provides the incentive. However, if quality is to be maintained and backlogged orders are to be kept to a minimum, sales must not exceed the ability of the manufacturing process to produce. Given the commission system, however, there is no incentive for the sales staff to take these limitations into account and to cooperate with manufacturing to secure the optimal amount of sales at any given time. As the result of Japanese competition, these defects have been recognized and American firms have realized that there must be greater cooperation among the units within the firm. In a business sense such cooperation is essential. What Bromiley and Cummings hypothesize is that greater cooperation among units within the firm is positively associated with trust. As they say, "Within a corporation, joint projects will tend to arise between divisions where managers have high levels of trust in each other."[32]

What holds true within a firm will hold true as various firms find it necessary to enter into joint ventures. However, to be a rational candidate for a joint venture, the firm has to be one that is trustworthy. Bromiley and Cummings hypothesize that firms with higher levels of trustworthiness will enter into more joint ventures. The rationale for this hypothesis is fairly clear. If one member of the joint venture fails to keep its end of the contract, behaves opportunistically, or provides a shoddy product, all in the joint venture will suffer. The customer will blame all alike. Thus, a trustworthy partner is the best partner in a business sense. Indeed, in this era of joint ventures, choosing a trustworthy partner may be one of the most important decisions a business firm may make.

Although Bromiley and Cummings have emphasized the reduction in transaction costs that can result from increased trust, many of their examples make the same point without the transaction cost perspective. As Ed Soule has pointed out to me, trust is essential for the possibility of certain business transactions. In correspondence Soule points out that many business deals really cannot be legally protected and must rely on trust. He cites cases of collaborative efforts where it is simply impossible to spell out all the rights and duties of the parties. I think this analysis would apply to many of the examples discussed by Bromiley and Cummings. Not only does lack of trust raise transaction costs, but lack of trust makes economic ventures like intra-firm cooperation or joint ventures difficult to undertake. Perhaps this point can be made most clearly by a discussion of virtual corporations.[33]

Trust is especially essential with a special kind of strategic alliance known as the virtual corporation. The virtual corporation is made up of constantly shifting members. It is the change in the composition of the virtual corporation that differentiates it from the traditional strategic alliance. With such flux, trust is even more essential. Indeed, several commentators have argued that trust is the key to the success of the virtual corporation.

As business commentator Charles Handy has said, "Trust is the heart of the matter. . . . Virtuality requires trust to make it work. Technology on its own is not enough."[34] As economists have noted, trust can be calculative. Each side trusts the other because it pays and since each side will interact many times in the future, there is good reason for each side to trust the other. But such trust is not rational in the virtual corporation because there is no guarantee of future contact. Sociologists argue that trust often develops as a social norm as people work together, but again that kind of trust will not work in the virtual corporation because there is no opportunity for stable norms of interaction to develop. Thus, the trust needed as a glue in the virtual corporation is the kind of trust associated with commitment. One strategy professor describes the kind of trust needed as "hard-core trust":

> Hard-core trustworthy exchange partners are trustworthy, independent of whether or not exchange vulnerabilities exist and independent of whether or not governance mechanisms exist. Rather, hard-core trustworthy exchange partners are trustworthy because that is who, or what, they are. . . . Strong form trust does not emerge from the structure of the exchange, but rather reflects the values, principles, and standards that partners bring to the exchange.[35]

It is this hard-core trust that is genuinely ethically based and it is this kind of trust that is absolutely required if virtual corporations are to survive.

Again, I wish to emphasize that these arguments are not simply consequentialist. What I am trying to show is that certain management practices are essential to the survival of the firm. To adopt practices which are inconsistent with those essential to the survival of the firm involves a pragmatic contradiction. And since managers have a moral obligation to promote the welfare of the firm, practices which involve a pragmatic contradiction in the sense of undermining the survival of the firm are immoral.

In summary, we have seen that being trusting and being trustworthy are characteristics that are essential in business transactions – all the more so in strongly competitive economies. Thus, to engage in activities that make one less trustworthy is to adopt a maxim that is pragmatically (volitionally) inconsistent.

Transition to Chapter 2

Thus far we have given an argument as to why certain actions, if taken in business, would be morally wrong. In general we have focused on prohibitions, on "thou shalt nots," on negative prohibitions such as "don't lie," "don't cheat," and "don't undermine trust." However, when we move from evaluating the actions or practices of a firm to describing how a firm ought to interact with its stakeholders, the second formulation of the categorical imperative will serve us especially well. Let us now turn to a discussion of stakeholder issues as we develop Kant's formulation of the principle that we are obligated to treat persons with respect.

Notes

1 Kenneth J. Arrow, "Business Codes and Economic Efficiency," *Public Policy* XXI (1973), p. 314.
2 Albert Carr, "Is Business Bluffing Ethical?" *Harvard Business Review* 46 (January/February 1968), pp. 145–6, 148.
3 Ibid., p. 145.
4 Immanuel Kant, *Foundations of the Metaphysics of Morals* 1785 (New York: Macmillan, 1990), p. 19.
5 Ibid., p. 38.
6 Christine M. Korsgaard, *Creating the Kingdom of Ends* (New York: Cambridge University Press, 1996), p. 85.
7 These examples have been discussed in many of my writings and this section of the book draws directly on those writings. See, for example, *Business Ethics* 2nd edn with Ronald Duska (Englewood Cliffs, NJ: Prentice Hall, 1990).
8 Korsgaard, *Creating the Kingdom of Ends*, p. 86.
9 Kant, *Foundations of the Metaphysics of Morals*, p. 41. Both Korsgaard and O'Neill see the importance of the "don't make an exception of yourself" interpretation of the universalization requirement.
10 John Rawls, *A Theory of Justice* (Cambridge, MA: Harvard University Press, 1971), pp. 497, 569.
11 Neela Banerjee, "Russian Concerns Find Glasnost Pays," *Wall Street Journal*, June 9, 1995, p. A6.
12 Myron Magnet, "The New Golden Rule of Business," *Fortune*, February 24, 1994, pp. 60–4.
13 David Woodruff, "Can Volkswagen Ride Out the Storm?" *Business Week*, November 25, 1996, pp. 34–6.
14 Kant, *Foundations of the Metaphysics of Morals*, pp. 40–1.
15 Christine M. Korsgaard, *Creating the Kingdom of Ends*, p. 78.
16 Ibid., pp. 96–7. Korsgaard notes that there are three possible interpretations of "contradiction" available. As this quotation shows,

Korsgaard thinks all the examples in the *Groundwork* can be adequately handled by the pragmatic interpretation.

17 Much more will be said about this distinction between perfect and imperfect duties in later chapters.

18 Onora O'Neill refers to a distinction between conceptual consistency and volitional consistency. See *Constructions of Reason* (New York: Cambridge University Press, 1989), p. 89.

19 Korsgaard, *Creating the Kingdom of Ends*, p. 92.

20 Onora O'Neill, *Constructions of Reason*, pp. 102–3.

21 Ibid., p. 92.

22 Ibid., pp. 101–2.

23 Korsgaard, *Creating the Kingdom of Ends*, p. 96.

24 Kenneth E. Boulding, "The Basis of Value Judgments in Economics," in *Human Values and Economic Policy*, ed. Sidney Hook (New York: New York University Press, 1967), p. 68.

25 As Ed Soule has reminded me there are different levels of trust. Soule distinguishes confidence from trust. In comments he provided me he points out that confidence is a matter of inductive reliance. He does not wonder about the quality of gas from the local Shell dealer because he has bought it there for years and is confident of its content. But he does not have a trusting attitude that normally accompanies genuine trust, He would not trust them in a situation where he is vulnerable to their discretionary power. Nonetheless, Soule agrees that trust in his sense of the word is essential for a number of business transactions.

26 Francis Fukuyama, *Trust* (New York: The Free Press, 1995), p. 152.

27 For an exceptionally well worked out theory of the benefits of trust in the firm, see David M. Kreps, "Corporate Culture and Economic Theory," in *Perspectives on Positive Political Economy*, ed. James E. Alt and Kenneth A. Shepsle (New York: Cambridge University Press, 1990), pp. 90–143.

28 This example is from Fukuyama, *Trust*, p. 153.

29 Of course, there are other explanations or partial explanations beside lack of trust. Ed Soule pointed out that the $800 toilet seat could be in part explained by government bureaucracy. However, lack of trust would certainly add to the effect caused by normal bureaucracy.

30 Philip Bromiley and Larry Cummings, "Transaction Costs in Organizations with Trust," in *Research on Negotiation in Organizations* 5, pp. 219–47.

31 Ibid., p. 236.

32 Ibid., p. 238.

33 The following argument is adapted from Thomas M. Jones and

Norman E. Bowie, "Moral Hazards on the Road to the Virtual Corporation," *Business Ethics Quarterly* 8 (March 1998), pp. 273–92.

34 Charles Handy, "Trust and the Virtual Organization," *Harvard Business Review* 73 (May–June 1995), p. 44.

35 Jay B. Barney and Mark B. Hansen, "Trustworthiness as a Source of Competitive Advantage," *Strategic Management Research Journal* 5 (1994), p. 179.

2

Treating the Humanity of Stakeholders as Ends Rather Than as Means Merely

Part of the power of Kant's ethics lies in the extent of its ability to answer questions that Kant himself did not consider. (Barbara Herman)

Introduction

If the average American has a second moral principle to supplement the Golden Rule, it is probably a principle that says we should respect people. Respecting people is thoroughly interwoven into the fabric of American moral life. There is no one in the business community that has challenged the respect for persons principle as a principle in business ethics the way Albert Carr challenged the application of the Golden Rule in business. Yet, ironically, many of the moral criticisms of business practice are directed against policies that do not respect persons, e.g., that business human relations policies often invade privacy or relegate people to dead-end jobs where they cannot grow. In addition, there is considerable controversy, even among ethicists, as to what a respect for persons principle requires.

In this chapter I shall develop Kant's respect for persons principle and show the implications of that principle for business practice. I believe that if Kant's respect for persons principle were honored, business practice would look very different. Thus, the application of Kantian ethics here calls for a fairly radical reform of business practice. Nonetheless, I shall argue that such reforms may actually enhance the bottom line, rather than hurt it as business people often suppose.

I want to begin with an example which, although oversimplified, represents a standard discussion of the application of Kant's respect for persons principle to business. After presenting the example, I shall provide Kant's justification of the respect for persons principle and, using contemporary scholarship, explain what Kant means by the principle. With that in hand I will be able to apply the principle to more complex business examples.

I recall from my undergraduate ethics class more than 30 years ago that we struggled with the issue of whether buying a product, like vegetables in the supermarket, violated the respect for persons requirement of the second formulation of the categorical imperative. In buying our groceries did we merely use the clerk who rang up our purchases on the register? The first issue to be decided was whether we treated the sales person as a thing. Somewhat naively we decided that we did not merely use people in business transactions because we could accomplish our goal – buying carrots or potatoes – but that we could still show respect to those on the other end of the transaction. A casual observer in a supermarket can usually distinguish those patrons who treat the cashiers with respect from those who do not.

Our "solution" in this undergraduate class did not address business exchanges that involve tradeoffs between human and nonhuman sources. Any introductory economics text establishes that the efficient producer is instructed always to rearrange capital, land, machines, and workers so that their proportional marginal productivity is equal. The requirement of equal proportional marginal productivity works as follows: If the price of machines rises with respect to labor, substitute labor for machines. If the price of labor rises with respect to machines, substitute machines for labor. Both substitutions are equivalent.[1]

At first glance it looks as if a Kantian would say that the two substitutions are not morally equivalent. The first is morally permissible; the second is not morally permissible. It looks as if the employees are used as a means merely for the enhancement of the profits of the stockholders. It is morally permissible to use machines that way but it is not morally permissible to use people that way. Unlike the grocery-store example, the managers who act on behalf of the stockholders are not in a personal face-to-face relationship with the employees and thus they cannot avoid the charge of merely using the employees by saying that in the transaction they treated the other party to the transaction with respect. It doesn't matter if the manager was nice to the employees when she laid them off – a fact of some importance in contemporary discussions of downsizing because many managers think that when they fire people in a nice way, as opposed to firing them cruelly, they are off the moral hook. It is morally better to be nice than to be cruel, but the real issue is whether the firing can be morally justified. How would a Kantian using the respect for persons principle justify these contentions? To answer that question some explanation of Kant's respect for persons principle is in order.

The Respect for Persons Principle

Kant's second formulation of the categorical imperative says "Act so that you treat humanity whether, in your own person or in that of another, always as an end and never as a means only."[2] Kant did not simply assert that human beings are entitled to respect; he had an elaborate argument for it. Human beings ought to be respected because human beings have dignity. For Kant, an object that has dignity is beyond price. That's what is wrong with the principle that says a manager should adjust the inputs of production to the point where the marginal productivity of each is equal. And further, the denial of dignity is what makes much downsizing unjust. In these cases, that which is without price, human beings, are treated as exchangeable with that which has a price. Human employees have a dignity that machines and capital do not have. Thus, managers cannot manage their corporate resources in the most efficient manner without violating the respect for persons principle – or so it seems. But why do persons possess a dignity which is beyond all price?

They have dignity because human beings are capable of autonomy and thus are capable of self-governance. As autonomous beings capable of self-governance they are also responsible beings, since autonomy and self-governance are the conditions for responsibility. A person who is not autonomous and who is not capable of self-governance is not responsible. That's why little children or the mentally ill are not considered responsible beings. Thus, there is a conceptual link between being a human being, being an autonomous being, being capable of self-governance, and being a responsible being.

Autonomous responsible beings are capable of making and following their own laws; they are not simply subject to the causal laws of nature. Anyone who recognizes that he or she is autonomous should recognize that he or she is responsible (that he or she is a moral being). As Kant argues, the fact that one is a moral being enables us to say that such a being possesses dignity.

> Morality is the condition under which alone a rational being can be an end in himself because only through it is it possible to be a lawgiving member in the realm of ends. Thus morality, and humanity insofar as it is capable of morality, alone have dignity.[3]

It is the fact that human beings are moral agents that makes them objects worthy of respect. As Hill puts it:

> [For Kant] moral conduct is the practical exercise of the noble capacity to be rational and self-governing, a capacity which sets us apart from the lower animals and gives us dignity. Kant's ethics is as much an ethics of self-esteem as it is an ethics of duty.[4]

Now as a point of logic a person who recognizes that he or she is responsible should ascribe dignity to anyone like him or her; that is, one should ascribe dignity to other creatures who have the capacity to be autonomous and responsible beings. As Kant says:

> Rational nature exists as an end in itself. Man necessarily thinks of his own existence in this way, and thus far it is a subjective principle of human actions. Also every other rational being thinks of his existence on the same rational ground which holds also for myself; thus it is at the same time an objective principle from which, as a supreme practical ground, it must be possible to derive all laws of the will.[5]

As I read Kant this is his argument for the necessity of including all other persons within the scope of the respect for persons principle (treating the humanity in a person as an end and never as a means merely). It is based on consistency. What we say about one case, namely ourselves, we must say about similar cases, namely about other human beings.

Up to this time I have said nothing about the rational nature of human beings, although the concept appears in the quotations from Kant that I have cited. There is a temptation to overemphasize Kant's rationalism here. Kant's focus is on the person as moral agent. Freedom and the ability to make laws (as opposed to being subjected to natural laws) are necessary conditions for moral agency. Thus, Kant is not a rationalist in the spirit of Descartes, Leibniz, or Spinoza. Rationalism is not a method to obtain truth about the world beyond sense experience. In the practical realm Kant clearly follows neither the deductive method of Spinoza nor the overly optimistic rationalism of Leibniz concerning the coincidence of virtue and happiness. Rather, for Kant, rationalism in the practical realm is the capacity to adopt maxims that pass the test of universality (the capacity to adopt maxims that would be unanimously accepted in an ideal kingdom of ends). The ability to be rational in that sense is a necessary condition for moral agency. A more formal way of putting this overall Kantian argument is as follows:

1   Someone is a moral agent if and only if she is free and has the ability to make laws.
2   Someone is free and has the ability to make laws if and only if she is rational.
3   Therefore if one is a moral agent, one is rational and if one is rational one is a moral agent.

But Kant's argument can work if all explicit reference to rationality is removed.[6] Kant begins the third section of the *Foundations* as follows:

> What else, then, can freedom of the will be but autonomy (the property of the will to be a law to itself?) The proposition that the will is a law to itself in all its actions, however, only expresses the principle that we should act according to no other maxim than that which can also have itself as a universal law for its object. And this is just the formula of the categorical imperative and the principle of morality. Therefore a free will and a will under moral laws are identical.[7]

Freedom and the ability to make laws are necessary and sufficient for moral agency. Moral agency is what gives people dignity. The importance of rationality comes when one explicates the meaning of freedom. Freedom is more than independence from causal laws. This is negative freedom. Freedom is also the ability to make laws that are universal and to act on those laws in the world. As Kant says:

> The sole principle of morality consists in independence from all material of the law (i.e., a desired object) and in the accompanying determination of choice by the mere form of giving universal law which a maxim must be capable of having. That independence, however, is freedom in the negative sense, while this intrinsic legislation of pure and thus practical reason is freedom in the positive sense.[8]

In commenting on Kant's views Onora O'Neill shows how reason functions in the Kantian moral framework. She first establishes that negative freedom is not sufficient for a morally responsible being. A notion of positive freedom is required as well.

> Positive freedom is more than independence from alien causes. It would be absent in lawless or random changes, although these are negatively free, since they depend on no alien causes. Since will is a mode of causality it cannot, if free at all, be merely negatively free, so it must work by nonalien causality . . . it [free will] must be a capacity for self-determination or autonomy.[9]

But how is self-determination free from alien causality possible? When a human being makes a law as the ground for his or her action, the basis for that law-making could either be inclination – such as concern with our happiness – or it could be from morality itself. But inclinations are from the world of sense and thus under the law of causality. Thus, if our legislation is based on inclination it is not really free. As Christine Korsgaard says, "Morality is the natural condition of a free will. The free will that puts inclination above morality sacrifices its freedom for nothing."[10]

If inclination is not to be the basis of our actions, what then remains is the form of the moral law which is rationality itself. Any law that is freely derived must be rational in the sense that it is universal, that is, willed universally by all free moral beings. Rationality in Kant's moral philosophy amounts to this requirement that the laws freely derived be capable of being willed universally. The fact that human beings in their capacity as free moral beings have this capability is a reason to accord them dignity. Thus, I agree with O'Neill when she says:

> He [Kant] argues not from reason to autonomy but from autonomy to reason. Only autonomous self-disciplining beings can act on principles that we have grounds to call principles of reason . . . it [the categorical imperative] is the fundamental strategy not just of morality but of all activity that counts as reasoned. The supreme principle of reason is merely the principle of thinking and acting on principles that can (not do!) hold for all.[11]

Thus, we have shown why Kant believes persons have dignity and in this world are the only beings who have dignity. Kant has thus grounded our obligation to treat humanity in a person as an end and never as a means merely. But what specific obligations follow from that general obligation? More specifically, what is the casuistry for applying the principle in a business context? I follow contemporary scholarship in arguing that respect for persons requires two steps and have divided this chapter accordingly. For example, O'Neill says:

> The maxim must not use them (negatively) as mere means, but also (positively) treat them as ends-in-themselves. Kant describes the first sort of failure as action on maxims to which no other could possibly consent, and the second as pursuit of ends another cannot share.[12]

Now we finally have the framework that can address the basic question for this chapter. How does the respect for persons principle apply in a corporate business setting? To illustrate how this Kantian principle can be applied, we will focus on the employer/employee relationship. We will use these two tests to show how managers may honor the respect for persons principle in the workplace. The strategy for this chapter is first to spell out some of the implications of the negative test when applied to managing employees, i.e., that they not be used. Of special interest will be the nature of the employment contract and the very contemporary problem of downsizing. I will then turn to the implications of the positive requirements. With respect to employees, providing meaningful work in a sense to be defined, is a good way to honor the positive requirement that the manager should treat the humanity in employees as an end.

Thus, this chapter focuses on the relation between managers and the firm's employees. Obviously, a full theory of the firm would spell out the requirements for dealing with all the corporate stakeholders in a way that respects the humanity in their persons. For reasons that will be provided below the respect for persons principle requires that no stakeholder should be coerced or deceived. With respect to customers, the nondeception requirement raises some extremely interesting questions regarding what counts as a deception. However, a detailed spelling out of the "treat the humanity in a person with respect" requirement would involve considerable overlap and repetition; it would also make this book too long. Since the manager/employee relation provides the possibility of a rich analysis, I have decided to focus on it. The reader is invited to extend this analysis to other corporate stakeholders.

Not Using Employees: Neither Coercion nor Deceit

The first step to respect the humanity in a person requires that a person should not be merely used. With respect to business ethics that means that a business relationship should be neither coerced nor deceptive. The general point has been made by Christine Korsgaard among others.

> According to the Formula of Humanity, coercion and deception are the most fundamental forms of wrongdoing to others – the roots of all evil. Coercion and deception violate the conditions of possible assent, and all actions which depend for their nature and efficacy on their coercive or deceptive character are ones that others cannot assent to. . . . Physical coercion treats someone's person as a tool; lying treats someone's *reason* as a tool. That is why Kant finds it so horrifying; it is a direct violation of autonomy.[13]

Kant's point is accepted by persons of nearly all political persuasions. Coercion and deception are a violation of one's negative freedom because they block a person from choosing ends she would have chosen had the coercion or deception not occurred.

Recall that this chapter began with a very simplified discussion of what it might mean to treat people with respect in a business relationship. Respect involves more than being nice to them, but are such business practices as massive downsizing disrespectful of workers in ways that would violate Kant's respect for the humanity in a person principle? Are the huge salaries that are given to chief executives in violation of Kant's principle? Conversations in the press and around the water cooler often reflect a positive answer to that question. But things are more complicated than they look at first glance. Economic actions are allegedly free actions voluntarily entered into. If both parties are also fully informed, then business transactions are neither coerced nor involve deception. They thus pass the two tests for negative freedom. Using the standard assumption that the employment relationship is a contractual one and further assuming that the employee has all the relevant knowledge regarding the relationship, then one could argue that the employee has accepted the fact that if the price of machinery becomes cheaper compared to the price of labor, then she has agreed that the manager may legitimately substitute a machine for her labor. Thus, one could say that workers know that they can be laid off if their labor becomes more expensive compared to machines. They accept the job knowing that and hence there is a perfectly understandable sense in which layoffs are agreed to. The employees are not used as means because they have freely consented to the conditions of their employment. There is neither coercion nor deception and thus the employees have not been used. (This argument resembles Hegel's argument that a criminal voluntarily accepts her punishment.)

The claim that the layoffs are indeed voluntary has been made by Oliver Williamson, who argues that the risks of a layoff have been incorporated in the salary contract. Wages include a payment for the risk of layoffs.[14] Only the risks of the stockholders have not been protected by a contract – the fact that entitles stockholders to their profits. Thus, someone following Williamson's reasoning could argue that not violating a person's negative freedom, that is, not interfering with a person's choices, is sufficient to honor Kant's respect for persons principle.

Is the argument that employment contracts, especially contracts that permit massive layoffs, are voluntary agreements sound? Several points should be made here. First, R. Edward Freeman and William Evan have shown that Williamson's argument is inadequate. First, Williamson has argued incorrectly that all other stakeholders except for stockholders can renegotiate the terms of their contracts and thus the stockholders need protection that the other parties to bilateral contracts with the firm do not need. Freeman and Evan show that individual stockholders do renegotiate every day in the stock market. Only if Williamson argues that stockholders in the aggregate cannot renegotiate and that each of the other stakeholders in the aggregate can renegotiate will his claim be plausible. But Freeman and Evan have argued that Williamson has given no coherent account of what a contract to stockholders in the aggregate would look like. Thus, we cannot be sure that stockholders differ from other stakeholders in this regard. Thus, an individual stockholder faces no more risk than an individual employee with respect to contracting.[15]

I would add to the Freeman–Evan argument by pointing out, first, that the individual employee faces risks that the individual stockholder does not. The individual stockholder can easily sell her shares. The individual employee cannot easily change jobs. And viewing the employment relation as a contract does not help much with the moral issue because an individual employee is virtually powerless in dealing with management – a fact that has led government to provide protection for individual workers through the right to unionization.

Second, some might argue that few layoffs are voluntary economic transactions because workers do not want to be laid off. A layoff is not like an ordinary commercial transaction, e.g., purchasing gasoline at a filling station. As an empirical matter the response of workers to the massive layoffs of downsizing counts against the theory that the layoffs are voluntary contracts freely entered into. The response of those laid off is hardly the response of one who has bought a lottery ticket and lost.

However, this argument will not get us very far. Defenders of the voluntary contract view could respond by arguing that the feelings of the laid-off employees are not determinate. Of course they do not want to be laid off, but they voluntarily accepted that risk nonetheless. (After all, those who are punished do not want to be punished, but they knowingly took the risk of punishment when they knowingly broke the law.)

But there is something to the argument. Consider a person who buys a car and has it repossessed because she cannot make the payments and the reason she cannot make the payments is because of something out of her control.[16] Layoffs, including the massive layoffs of downsizing, are hardly the fault of the employees. If blame is to be placed, perhaps it should be placed on management who hired too many employees in the first place.

Another way to address the problem is to focus on the institution of capitalism as it is currently practiced rather than on the specific transactions between an individual employee and the firm she works for. This approach has in fact been taken by Onora O'Neill.

> What could be more paradigmatic of an offer that can be refused than an offer of employment that is, as they say in wage negotiations, "on the table"? If we argue that such offers are coercive or deceptive, we must take a broader view of maxims, and judge not the principles that particular would-be employees have in mind but the principles that guide the institution of employment in a capitalist system. The underlying principle of capitalist employment, whatever that may be, might be judged to use some as means or fail to treat them as persons, even where individuals' intentions fail in neither way.[17]

O'Neill's argument, and ones similar to it, presupposes that a coherent account can be given of the notion of institutional coercion. The key to a coherent account is the plausibility of an account of intentionality that could apply to institutions. Interestingly, critics of the functionalist theory of institutions, including such scholars as David Lewis, Jon Elster, and John Rawls, support intentional theories. Philosophers such as Denis Arnold are currently at work on developing the insights of these scholars in a way that enables us to talk meaningfully of institutional coercion. Arnold looks to the formal and informal policies of an institution as well as to its leaders to determine whether or not certain institutional activities coerce individuals.[18] Thus, let us proceed with O'Neill's analysis. Indeed, let us broaden O'Neill's idea to include the notion that institutions can deceive as well as coerce. What arguments can be given to show that capitalism either coerces or deceives and thus violates the

Kantian provision that people should not be treated merely as a means?

The coercion argument might proceed as follows: During one's productive years, there is hardly a choice between working and not working. If all viable work options must include acceptance of the risk of layoff, then it could be plausibly argued that the employee does not voluntarily accept but is forced to accept an employment contract where layoffs are permitted. There is some precedent here in business law. In a widely accepted New Jersey Supreme Court case the warranties offered by the automobile industry were struck down by the Court using a similar argument. Here is the language of the Court:

> The warranty before us is a standardized form designed for mass use. It is imposed upon the automobile consumer. He takes it or leaves it, and he must take it to buy an automobile. No bargaining is engaged in with respect to it. The form warranty is not only standard with Chrysler but, as mentioned above, it is the uniform warranty of the Automobile Manufacturer Association. . . . Because his [the consumer's] capacity for bargaining is so grossly unequal, the inexorable conclusion which follows is that he is not permitted to bargain at all. He must take or leave the automobile on the warranty dictated by the maker.[19]

Now how close is the analogy between the standard automobile warranty and many of the employment conditions of the standard wage contract, e.g., the acceptance of layoffs on economic grounds such as a fall in the demand for the product, an increase in the price of labor, or simply on grounds of efficiency to increase the return to the stockholders? Those who find the analogy to be close would argue that the layoff provisions which are implicitly accepted in most labor contracts are dictated just as the warranty is dictated. There are few competitors to offer a better deal. For those who see the analogy this way, unhesitatingly laying off employees to enhance profits still appears to be a violation of the respect for persons principle.

I admit that this matter is extremely controversial. However, if the employment-at-will provision of the standard labor contract in many industries is like the warranty in our court case, and if being

forced to accept a contract provision because one is without significant bargaining power is an acceptable account of coercion, then
the standard employment-at-will provision in many industries fails
to pass the Kantian test. It does not respect the humanity of the
employee. Thus, on Kantian grounds some alternative must be
found.

Before exploring some alternatives let us address the issue of
deception in the standard labor contract. One of the real problems
in labor management discussions is the existence of asymmetrical
information. The management knows far more about the firm's
finances than the employees do. Given this asymmetry it is easy for
management to deceive employees regarding the necessity for certain management policies, such as layoffs or salary freezes. To the
extent that management does use information in this way they are in
violation of Kant's respect for persons principle.

However, there is no business necessity for such asymmetrical
information. Suppose management sees that a new machine can
accomplish a task more cheaply than human workers can. Rather
than automatically replacing labor with machines, the manager in a
capitalist firm could provide the employees with full information on
the financial situation the firm faces and then consult with the
employees as to how to proceed. There are possibilities besides
involuntary layoffs. The employees might agree to pay cuts, a
reduced work week, or pay cuts that would finance an early retire-
ment scheme or perhaps retraining. Both the deception charge and
the coercion charge could be avoided if the employees really were
fully informed and really were able to choose.

In what follows I shall describe a number of business practices
that are an improvement on the traditional labor contract in that
they are more in conformity with Kant's respect for persons principle. In describing these practices I am not saying that Kantian
moral theory requires them. Kantian ethics is not that specific and,
as you recall from chapter 1, is not designed to be. Actions or
practices that pass the test of the categorical imperative are permitted, not required. Furthermore, some of the practices that I describe
as improvements on traditional labor contracts are still not in full
conformity with the categorical imperative. In those cases I shall
indicate how those practices may be brought into conformity with
the categorical imperative.

Business Practices That Reduce or Remove Coercion and Deception

Open book management

As pointed out above one of the chief difficulties with the traditional employment contract is the existence of asymmetrical information. It is management that traditionally has the financial information that would enable workers to judge whether the overall labor contract in the firm is fair. The existence of asymmetrical information presents a temptation to deceive, since the deception would be hard to discover. We need institutional arrangements which reduce or eliminate asymmetrical information. One exemplary method that deserves special attention because it enables a firm to eliminate asymmetrical information is open book management. It was developed by Jack Stack at the Springfield Manufacturing Company. Stack and his company won a prestigious business ethics award for open book management. In addition to his own book, *The Great Game of Business*, other books on open book management, including one popularized by John Case, have been published and open book management has subsequently been adopted with appropriate modification by a number of firms including Intel, Allstate Business Insurance, Herman Miller, Jenkins Diesel Power, Foldcraft, Manco, and Rhino Foods. The underlying philosophy of open book management is that persons should be treated as responsible autonomous beings. A precondition of such treatment is that employees have the information needed to make responsible decisions. Case calls this "empowerment with brains."

Under open book management employees are given all the financial information about the company. They are also under a profit-sharing plan where what they make is in large part determined by the profit of the company. With complete information and the proper incentive, employees behave responsibly without the necessity of layers of supervision.

How does open book management do what it does? The simplest answer is this. People get a chance to act, to take responsibility, rather than just doing their job. . . . No supervisor or department head can anticipate or handle all . . . situations. A company that hired enough managers to do so would go broke from the overhead. Open book management gets people on the job doing things right. And it teaches them to make smart decisions . . . because they can see the impact of their decisions on the relevant numbers.[20]

The adoption of practices like open book management would go far toward correcting the asymmetrical information that managers possess and that gives rise to the charge that the employment contract is often deceptive. Any time the firm faces a situation that might involve the layoff of employees, employees as well as managers would have access to all the relevant information. Deception in such circumstances would be much more difficult.

But access to information is not enough. Labor contracts must not be coercive either. We need institutional changes and changes in practice that lessen layoffs for reasons other than the cause. After all it is the threat of arbitrary layoff as exemplified in the doctrine of employment at will that makes employees accept conditions of employment they would not accept if the threat of arbitrary layoff did not exist. The doctrine of employment at will says that in the absence of a contract stating otherwise and so long as federal and state labor law is followed, e.g., no racial discrimination, then a person can be fired for any reason or for no reason. No Kantian could accept a policy that allows for arbitrary dismissal. And some companies have adopted policies that protect against layoffs and more positively that insure that all employees share in the producer's surplus, i.e., productivity gains.

Each year Fortune identifies the 100 best companies to work for in America. Among the characteristics listed as defining criteria of good companies to work for are no layoff policies. Eighteen companies on the 1998 Fortune list had no layoff policies. These companies were Amgen, Baldor Electric, Baptist Health Systems, Cisco Systems, Deere, Erie Insurance, FedEx, H.B. Fuller, Granite Rock, Great Plains, Harley Davidson, S.C.Johnson Wax, Lands' End, Herman Miller, Southwest Airlines, Steelcase, Wegmans, and Worthington Industries. Three other companies were identified as companies that go to great length to avoid downsizing. Hewlett-Packard which ranked number 10 overall in the 1998 Fortune survey has had a long history of no layoffs. The other two companies were Hallmark Cards and the gigantic 3M Corporation. During the severe recession of 1983–4 the NuCor Corporation, a steel maker, faced a severe decline in revenues. Rather than lay off workers, all employees (including the CEO) were put on two or three day work weeks with a corresponding cut in pay. I am not sure if the NuCor decision was a management decision strictly or was a shared decision. But the employees responded in a way that indicates they preferred that decision to the traditional layoff policy. When economic conditions improved and the company went back to full shifts, morale was outstanding. The increased productivity that followed the recession was largely attributed to the sharing of the pain that had occurred.[21]

Yet another criticism of capitalism is that it is inherently deceptive because employees are deceived about the nature of the wage contract. Some claim that workers are deceived and hence cheated because they do not realize that they are not paid the full value of what they contribute to the firm. As stated this argument is economically naive. The profits of a firm result from the interaction of all the factors of production. There is a producer's surplus that results from the beneficial interaction of all the factors of production. As a starting point it seems fair to say that no one factor has a right to all the gains in productivity. Beyond that, how those gains should be distributed is a contestable issue of fairness. Recently, as a matter of fact, many of the gains from increases in productivity in the United States during the 1980s and 1990s have gone mostly to corporate executives and to the owners of capital. For example, in the USA the ratio of the salary of the highest paid to the salary of the lowest paid person in the firm has increased dramatically. Also the percentage returns to capital far exceed the percentage increase in wages. For example, the 1997 *Business Week* report on executive compensation points out that the CEO receives average compensation 209 times greater than the compensation of the average factory worker. The average 1996 raise for a factory worker was 3 percent. The average 1996 total compensation for a CEO rose 54 percent to $5,781,300. Even *Business Week* described CEO compensation as out of control.[22] By the way, corporate profits were up substantially but only by 11 percent. The Standard and Poor's 500 stock index was up substantially as well, but at 23 percent it was still well below the average 54 percent raise for CEOs. *Business Week* reaches the same conclusion regarding fairness that I do:

As once outsize options packages become the norm, many CEO's are taking the lion's share. Far smaller gains are going to managers and other key employees. The disturbing message: The CEO deserves nearly all the credit for the company's success. . . . Companies use options in part to align executives' interests with shareholders. But they also favor them because – unlike other forms of pay – they never show up on an income statement. Instead starting this year, companies must footnote them in their annual reports.[23]

So the issues of deception and coercion are still relevant. Few fully informed workers with alternative opportunities for employment would accept the distribution of the profits of increased productivity that has occurred in the past generation.

Profit sharing

However, the traditional capitalist wage structure could be changed. There could be less dependence on a fixed wage and more use of a profit-sharing plan. Profit-sharing plans that extend to the entire workforce allow everyone to share in the gains that result from increasing productivity. In theory they also allow everyone to share in the risks of an economic downturn. Indeed, profit-sharing plans are becoming far more common. John Case indicates that more than 10,000 companies have a formal employee stock option plan (ESOP) and that another 4,000 or so have another kind of stock plan for employees. An estimated 15 million people work in employee-ownership companies.[24] In describing some of these plans I wish to emphasize that their terms vary and that some are more in conformity with the categorical imperative than others. I also re-mind the reader that Kantian ethics does not require a certain plan. Rather, Kantian ethics provides guidelines for the creation of such plans – guidelines that if followed would enable the plan to be in conformity with the categorical imperative.

One of the more successful publicly held companies in the USA, Starbucks, went public in 1993. The CEO of Starbucks, Howard Schultz, explicitly rejects the notion that employees are interchange-able with machines or with each other. Rather, employees are the reason for the success of Starbucks. David Bollier, writing about Starbucks, says:

Schultz never accepted the flawed logic that workers were simply interchangeable components of a business nor did he believe that high turnover was more cost-effective than providing benefits to employees who contributed value to the company.[25]

With that Kantian perspective as a given, Starbucks created a variation on the traditional ESOP with Starbuck's "Bean Stock" option plan. Under an ESOP you buy shares in the firm. Under the "Bean Stock" an employee is entitled to buy a certain number of shares in the future at the price in effect at the time the option is offered. It is reported that an employee with ten years' service at Starbucks will secure stock options worth three times their salary.[26]

Another example is the Intel Corporation which paid $820 million in 1996 profit-sharing and retirement contributions to its 48,500 employees worldwide. Intel has also announced a stock option plan for all of its employees, making it one of the few companies that provides a form of compensation normally reserved for executives to all. That amount is one of the most lucrative bonuses ever paid by a corporation to employees. The $214 million in profit sharing was the equivalent of about 27 days of pay for every employee. For an entry level employee making $25,000 a year, the bonuses could increase pay by about $8,000.[27] Craig Barrett, president designate, said, "This outstanding year would not have been possible without the remarkable efforts of Intel employees. Our bonus and profit-sharing plan are one way we can recognize their significant achievement."[28]

One plan that deserves special attention is that of the H.B. Fuller Company, a Fortune 500 publicly owned corporation with headquarters in St Paul, Minnesota. The plan is called Profit Share Plus. Profit Share Plus is really a bonus plan where a portion of the bonus is paid in cash and a portion is given in shares of stock. A unique feature of the plan is that it is offered to Fuller employees in foreign countries and is based on worldwide financial results and individual employee performance; in fact, it was the first plan of its type in the world. Significantly, the plans in countries other than the USA are designed to come as close to the American plans as the rules of foreign governments allow. The program was started in nine countries in 1992 (Australia, Austria, Belgium, Canada, Germany, Spain, Sweden, United Kingdom, and the United States) and has now been added in four countries that have never had profit-sharing bonus plans (Costa Rica, Hong Kong, New Zealand, and Taiwan) as well as in eleven other countries. An implementation schedule is in place that will add another seven countries. Only government obstacles in other countries prevent the plan from being implemented in the other seven countries where H.B. Fuller has facilities.

The plan is managed extremely conservatively and is on sound financial ground. The plan is not leveraged, which means that the stock is purchased from the market at the time of distribution. It is not a pension benefit swap. All employees participate and thus become owners of H.B. Fuller stock. The plan "kicks in" after minimum earnings goals are reached (2.7 percent of worldwide sales), which insures affordability. The value of the stock is available only upon separation of employment.

For profit-sharing plans, ESOPs, and their variations to be fully morally acceptable, certain other conditions need to be met. One of the major difficulties of most stock option plans is that they are not available to most employees. They tend to be a perk of top management. This practice only exacerbates the growing income gap between employer and employees. To meet the challenge posed by the inequality argument, all – or at least all full-time employees – should be eligible for the plan. And Fortune seems to agree, since stock options for all employees is listed as one of the criteria for a good company to work for. Companies cited favorably in that regard in the 1998 survey include Amgen, Cisco Systems, First Tennessee Bank, General Mills, W.L.Gore, Great Plains Software, McCormick, Merck, Procter and Gamble, Intel, and Microsoft.

The biggest problem from the ethical perspective with ESOPs and other profit-sharing plans is that management dictates the terms and that the information on which management's decision was based is not made available to the employee. Since the employee has none of the information on which the decision was based, a condition of extreme information asymmetry exists which makes the employee vulnerable to deception. In addition, some might argue that there is still an element of coercion to accept the terms of the ESOP. Thus, to fully avoid the charges of coercion and deception, the terms of these plans would have to be freely accepted by the employees and this acceptance should in turn rest on full financial information. As we shall see later in this chapter and in the next, participation in making the rules and policies that affect one is another requirement of Kantian morality.

One profit-sharing plan that meets these moral requirements is called the Scanlon plan. Scanlon plans were the brainchild of Joseph Scanlon, who began working with companies to institutionalize them in the 1930s. After Scanlon's death in 1956, his ideas were championed by Frederick Lesieur. Under a Scanlon plan a business firm commits itself to share the gains of productivity with the employees. This is done by a formula which uses a ratio between the total person-power costs of the enterprise and a measure of output such as total sales or the value added by manufacture. Any improvement in that standard ratio goes to the employees in a range from 20–100 percent, although 70 percent is typical.

What is additionally significant is the management philosophy that underlies Scanlon plans. As we shall see, this management philosophy is Kantian. First, it is participative and cooperative. There are formal committees that consider suggestions for improvement of the ratio. But more importantly there are many informal meetings of four or five people that can arise spontaneously and take place on the shop floor. One observer has described the perspective as follows:

> The distinctive potential contribution of the human being in contrast to the machine at *every level of the organization* stems from his capacity to think, to plan, to exercise judgment, to be creative, to direct and control his own behavior.[29]

Thus, Scanlon plans respect the autonomy of employees and help them to exercise their rational and creative capacities: just what is required on a Kantian theory. Scanlon plans encourage and reward the distinctively human contribution to business.

An Objection and Replies

But are profit-sharing plans that provide this level of employee autonomy and access to information practical? Wouldn't firms that avoided coercion and deception be at a competitive disadvantage? Moreover, economists frequently claim that these cooperative plans are doomed to failure because of the tendency for human beings to "free-ride." The argument goes as follows: In any group project, each individual in the group is tempted to contribute less than she could and still get the gains that result from the cooperative activity of others. Since everyone reasons that way the productivity of the group is much less than where people's individual contribution can be recognized and rewarded accordingly. Professors are familiar with this free-riding problem when they make group assignments and the group receives the grade. Some students always complain that members of the group are free-riding. These students argue that it is not fair that those who free-ride get the same grade as those who do not. The free-riding problem undermines group cooperation both in classroom team projects and in the business world. Thus, isn't the ethical analysis in obvious danger of being shipwrecked on the shoals of economic reality?

I think not for many reasons. The economic argument depends on a certain conception of human nature, namely that everyone is a utility maximizer who seeks his own individual interest. However, this picture of human nature is at best only partially correct. There is considerable empirical evidence that contradicts what economic theory would predict. One can begin by citing the existence of highly successful firms that are organized cooperatively, even employee owned. A number of important examples are found in Jeffrey Pfeffer's *Competitive Advantage Through People*.[30] Additional evidence is found in a 1990 Brookings Institute study which charted the relation between various compensation plans and productivity. Profit sharing and gain sharing are most likely to succeed when they are combined with a high degree of worker participation.[31] One paper in that study by David I. Levine and Laura D'Andrea Tyson evaluated their empirical results as follows:

> Participation is more likely to have a long term effect on productivity when it involves decisions related to shop floor daily life, when it involves substantive decision-making rights rather than purely consultative arrangements (for example, quality circles), and when it occurs in an environment characterized by a high degree of employee commitment and employee–management trust. . . . On the basis of several participatory arrangements . . . we identify four features of a firm's industrial relations system needed to maintain employee support for participation. These features are gain sharing, long

term employment relations, measures to build group cohesiveness, and guaranteed individual rights for employees.[32]

Thus, if Levine and Tyson are right there is an exact congruence between what Kantian morality requires, namely that the employees participate in the adoption of compensation plans, and what prudence dictates, namely enhancing the chance that profit sharing really does lead to greater productivity.

In addition, there is considerable laboratory evidence that indicates that people do not free-ride nearly as much as the theory predicts, especially when there is even minimal contact among the participants in the group project. The evidence is so conclusive that an article has been published in a scholarly journal entitled "Economists Free Ride, Does Anyone Else?"[33] Finally, even where free-riding is found it is heavily influenced by culture. Christopher Earley has found that less individualistic cultures than the USA's experience less free-riding.[34] Thus, free-riding is not a fact of human nature as many economists assume, but is rather culturally determined. All of this lends support to the view that organizing business firms so that they are more cooperative is not utopian. Business firms that are organized cooperatively in the ways discussed above are less vulnerable to ethical objections and these best practices are adoptable by all firms.

Brief summary

A brief summary is in order. In this chapter I have argued that labor contracts and labor practices cannot contain standardized provisions that are detrimental to employees but which they must accept if they are to obtain employment at all. Moreover, I have contended that employees should participate in making the employment policies that affect them. Thus, when an economic crisis looms, employees must have some choice in the policy decision. One way to insure that a firm's employment contract is not coercive or deceptive is to have a profit-sharing plan, allow employees a voice in determining the nature of the plan, and provide employees with the necessary information for making a good decision. In the section that follows I shall argue that the Kantian requirement that humanity in a person be respected does require that people participate in making the rules and policies that govern them. Moreover, in the next chapter I shall argue that a business firm that passes the tests of Kantian morality must be far more democratic than the traditional business firm is today. I delay further discussion of that issue until the next chapter, which focuses on the organizational structure of the firm.

Positive Freedom and Meaningful Work: Respecting the Humanity in a Person

Lack of coercion and deception is not always sufficient for treating those in a business relationship with respect. On occasion we are obliged to act positively to further their humanity. This is because we must not only not use people but we must also treat them as ends in themselves. To treat a person as an end itself sometimes requires that we do more than merely refrain from coercion or deception; it requires that we take some positive action to help a person. This is required both by the respect for persons formulation of the categorical imperative, by some of Kant's own writings on the nature of work, and by Kant's imperfect duty of beneficence to help others.

I now argue that an obvious way a business firm can honor its obligation is to provide meaningful work. For this argument I shall build on Kant's characterization of positive freedom. One contemporary Kant scholar who has most persuasively articulated the Kantian theory of positive freedom is Thomas E. Hill, Jr. As we said earlier, negative freedom for Kant is the ability to act independently of determination by alien causes. Positive freedom is the autonomy persons have to be a law unto themselves.

The task before us is to derive the meaningful work requirement from Kant's notion of positive freedom. In deriving this requirement, I make use of Hill's interpretation of the phrase "humanity as an end in itself." Hill begins his analysis by asking what does morality require if we are to treat humanity as an end in itself? To answer this question, we must know what Kant means by humanity. The popular answer is that Kant equates humanity with our capacity for rational thought. But although rationality in the sense of being bound by the laws of reason is surely part of what Kant means by humanity, it is not the only part. Based on his examination of the Kantian texts, Hill argues that humanity includes the following capacities:

1   The capacity and disposition to act on the basis of reasons.
2   The capacity to act on principles of prudence and efficiency (hypothetical imperatives) so long as these hypothetical imperatives do not contradict categorical imperatives.
3   The power to set any end whatsoever which includes the "ability to see future consequences, adopt long-range goals, resist immediate temptation, and even to commit oneself to ends for which one has no sensuous desire."
4   The capacity to accept categorical imperatives.
5   "Some ability to understand the world and to reason abstractly."[35]

Assuming that Hill is right, it is a requirement of morality that people treat other people in ways that respect these capacities, for that is what Kant means by treating humanity as an end in itself.

But Hill's account still focuses solely on our rational capacities. Some contemporary commentators have gone further in specifying what it means to respect the humanity in the person of another. For textual support they begin by citing the two examples of moral duties from the *Foundations of the Metaphysics of Morals*, specifically the imperfect duties to develop one's talents and give aid to the needy.[36] These commentators then indicate that additional textual support is available from the *Metaphysics of Morals*. There Kant explicitly says that being indifferent to someone does not treat him as a means merely (merely use them). But being indifferent does not treat that person as an end in itself. That is why, for Kant, not using people is not sufficient for respecting them in the way morality requires. In part two of the *Metaphysics of Morals* Kant develops his theory of our obligations of virtue, that is of our obligations not backed by force of law. Kant argues that one has both a duty of perfection to oneself and a duty to promote the happiness of others. He asks: "What are the ends which are at the same time duties? They are these: one's own perfection and the happiness of others."[37] In an elaboration on our duty to promote the happiness of others

Kant argues that each must be concerned with the physical welfare of others and with their moral well-being.[38] Thus, our duty of beneficence requires that we do more to respect the humanity in a person than simply respect the rational capacities that people have. Let us take respecting a person's rational capacities as a necessary condition but not a sufficient condition for respecting the humanity in a person. At some level we must be concerned about their happiness as well.

I think we must be careful about how broadly we interpret this notion of happiness. Kant is basically concerned to show that we have an obligation to be concerned with the humanity of others. Thus, our primary concern is with the rational capacities that Hill has identified, as well as our rational well-being. One must also be concerned about the physical welfare of others and with their moral development. But one has no further obligation to make them happy. What I intend to show is that work should be constructed so far as possible to protect and support the humanity in each worker as defined above. That is the maxim which the moral manager would adopt.

Before applying Kant's imperatives regarding treating humanity as an end in itself, a few more clarifying textual comments are necessary. What is the nature of our positive duty to promote the happiness of others or – in our more restricted language – to promote the positive freedom of another? Kant believed it is an imperfect duty in the sense that we do not need to help another on every occasion where it is possible to do so. Using the schemata provided by Hill,[39] the duty to help another is subject to the following conditions:

1   One cannot promote the happiness or positive freedom of another by violating a perfect duty. For example, one cannot lie to promote the happiness of another.
2   One must have as a maxim that one will promote the happiness or positive freedom of others.
3   Nonetheless, for any given occasion where I could promote the happiness of another I have the option of not promoting it in this case.
4   I must actually promote the happiness of others on various occasions.

5   These acts of benevolence must be done from the appropriate moral motive.

But how as a practical matter should this be done? Onora O'Neill indicates that any application of the duty of beneficence involves a certain tension between love and respect.[40] On the one hand, we must be concerned with the activities that others would adopt in order to be happy. This is the love part. On the other hand, we cannot impose on them our views of what activities they should engage in to make them happy. That is the respect part. In paternalism, love is carried too far at the expense of respect.

> Policies of respect must recognize that the other's maxims and projects are *their* maxims and projects. They must avoid merely taking over or achieving the aims of these maxims and projects, and must allow others the "space" in which to pursue them for themselves.[41]

Let us apply all this to the firm. Employers must not coerce (violate the negative liberty) of their employees; this duty is a perfect one. Moreover, employers have an imperfect duty to adopt a maxim to be concerned with the positive liberty of their employees; that is, with their moral well-being and physical welfare. Of special concern are the rational capacities identified by Hill. Management practice should be such that it strengthens, rather than weakens, the rational capacities of employees.

With respect to the general welfare or happiness of employees, managers also have an imperfect obligation to be concerned with the physical welfare of employees and to do nothing that impedes their moral development. Managers must allow employees the latitude to pursue their individual conceptions of happiness in accordance with their own desires. It should be noted that firms should not act paternalistically. For example, there is nothing wrong with a company having a gym for the use of employees during lunch time or after work, but there is something wrong with a company requiring that employees use the gym so that they become more healthy. It should be noted that many companies behave in a paternalistic fashion and although some of these practices may be considered enlightened, a Kantian would reject them on moral grounds. This fact reminds us that the Kantian moral perspective does not simply endorse a hodgepodge of "enlightened" management practices.

What I shall now argue is that adopting the maxim of providing positive liberty for employees can be honored if the employers provide meaningful work. This is because spelling out the content of positive liberty as we have done here provides a reasonable account of the normative conditions for meaningful work. For a Kantian, meaningful work is work that allows the worker to exercise her autonomy and independence, that enables the worker to develop her rational capacities, that provides a wage sufficient for physical welfare, that supports the moral development of the employee, and that is not paternalistic in the sense of interfering with the worker's conception of how she wishes to obtain happiness.

Although much of my argument will be based on the implications of Kant's moral theory when applied to the business world, Kant himself had a few explicit things to say about the nature of work.

Kant's Reflections on Work

First, Kant argues that work is necessary for the development of selfhood.

> Life is the faculty of spontaneous activity, the awareness of all our human powers. Occupation gives us this awareness. . . . Without occupation man cannot live happily. If he earns his bread, he eats it with greater pleasure than if it is doled out to him. . . . Man feels more contented after heavy work than when he has done no work; for by work he has set his powers in motion.[42]

Somewhat surprisingly, perhaps, Kant endorses wealth and the pleasures it brings. Moreover, wealth contributes to self-respect because it provides independence. To work simply in order to make money is to display the vice of miserliness, a vice which is even worse than than avarice. So long as work is required to make money so that one can provide for one's needs and pleasures and in so doing make oneself independent, work has value. Selected comments of Kant's will establish his view:

A man whose possessions are sufficient for his needs is well-to-do. . . . All wealth is means . . . for satisfying the owner's wants, free purposes and inclinations. . . . By dependence on others man loses in worth, and so a man of independent means is an object of respect. . . . But the miser finds a direct pleasure in money itself, although money is nothing but a pure means. . . . The spendthrift is a lovable simpleton, the miser a detestable fool. The former has not destroyed his better self and might face the misfortune that awaits him with courage, but the latter is a man of poor character.[43]

This selection is from Kant's brief remarks, which amount to less than ten pages and represent student notes from his lectures on ethics in the 1770s before he had written his more famous and critical works on ethical theory. Nonetheless, they provide a starting point for a Kantian theory of meaningful work and for the obligations of a firm with respect to providing it.

So long as business firms provide jobs that provide sufficient wealth, they contribute to the independence and thus to the self-respect of persons. For a Kantian, the true contribution of capitalism would be that it provides jobs that help provide self-respect. The purchase of consumer goods in an affluent society often simply provides pleasure. Having a job provides the means for securing pleasure and the independence necessary for self-respect. If it is true that our current welfare programs make people dependent, Kant would consider them a great evil. And a capitalism that provides jobs that do not provide sufficient income for independence is also morally flawed. Kant would be as concerned as we are about the scope of corporate downsizing and the loss of jobs that do not provide a living wage.[44]

Kant evaluated thrift on moral rather than economic grounds. He said:

Thrift is care and scruple in the spending of one's substance. It is no virtue; it requires neither skill nor talent. A spendthrift of good taste requires much more of these qualities than does he who merely saves; an arrant fool can save and put money aside; to spend one's money with refinement on pleasure needs knowledge and skill, but there is no cleverness in accumulating by thrift. The thrifty who acquire their wealth by saving, are as a rule small minded people.[45]

Alan Greenspan take note. It would be stretching the point to claim that Kant is a precursor of Keynes, but it is clear that wealth for Kant is something to be used to meet our material needs and that its moral value is in providing us with the independence needed to meet our material needs. In the *Metaphysical Principles of Virtue* Kant says: "Therefore become thrifty so you do not become destitute."[46] Somewhat surprisingly, Kant does not follow Luther and Protestant ethics here. Weber could not cite Kant in favor of his thesis. There is no intrinsic merit to saving itself. Savings are to be used to support one's autonomy in the material world. I say "surprisingly," because Kant's ethics was strongly influenced by German pietism, yet on this point is not consistent with it.

Although Kant's explicit remarks on work are rather limited, nonetheless I believe the following ideas concerning the obligation of the manager to employees have explicit warrant in the Kantian texts:

1   A corporation can be considered moral in the Kantian sense only if the humanity of employees is treated as an end and not as a means merely.

2   If a corporation is to treat the humanity of employees as an end and not as a means merely, then a corporation should honor the self-respect of the employees.

3   To honor the employees' self-respect, the employees must have a certain amount of independence as well as the ability to satisfy a certain amount of their desires. Thus, the corporation should allow a certain amount of independence and make it possible for employees to satisfy a certain amount of their desires.

4   In an economic system people achieve independence and satisfaction of their desires using their wages which they earn as employees.

5   Thus, a corporation should pay employees a living wage, that is, a wage sufficient to provide a certain amount of independence and some amount of satisfaction of desires.[47]

A few qualifications are required to the above argument. What if market conditions are such that a company cannot provide a living wage for certain jobs? Supply and demand for labor for certain tasks may be in equilibrium at a point below a living wage. Is a business firm morally required on Kantian grounds to pay the living wage even though doing so would make the firm uncompetitive and endanger its survival? No, for several reasons. First, I have not argued that meaningful work as it is spelled out here is an absolute requirement of Kantian morality. Rather, providing meaningful work is one possible and rather effective way for a firm to honor the requirement that it respect the humanity of its employees and the imperfect obligation of beneficence. However, if the labor market does not permit a firm to honor the obligation of beneficence in this way, it is not required to do so. Although I cannot argue for it here, I would maintain that in such situations there is an obligation on the part of the state that it pass minimum wage laws and that it serve as an employer of last resort.

Although this is as much as one can say about meaningful work given the Kantian text, I believe a Kantian can say more about the moral value of work than that it gives us independence and thus self-respect.[48] By combining Kant's explicit remarks on work with the rest of his ethical theory and with the insights of recent commentators on Kant, I believe a Kantian would endorse the following principles of meaningful work. These principles would be an effective way to honor the requirement that the humanity in employees be respected.

1   Meaningful work is work that is freely chosen and provides opportunities for the worker to exercise autonomy on the job.
2   The work relationship must support the autonomy and rationality of human beings. Work that unnecessarily deadens autonomy or that undermines rationality is immoral.[49]
3   Meaningful work is work that provides a salary sufficient for the worker to exercise her independence and provides for her physical well-being and the satisfaction of some of her desires.
4   Meaningful work is work that enables a person to develop her rational capacities.
5   Meaningful work is work that does not interfere with a person's moral development.

6   Meaningful work is work that is not paternalistic in the
       sense of interfering with the worker's conception of how
       she wishes to obtain happiness.

I remind the reader that these are normative conditions for
meaningful work derived from Kantian moral philosophy. They
need not be descriptive of how employees would define meaningful
work, although as a matter of fact I believe the empirical evidence
shows that there would be considerable overlap.

Meaningful Work and Contemporary Business

Although a Kantian philosophy of the workplace is still the exception rather than the rule, some organizational theorists and individual companies are committed to providing more meaningful
work to employees. Jeffrey Pfeffer has argued that firms can gain a
competitive advantage if they focus on their employees. He identifies 16 practices for managing people successfully: (1) employment
security; (2) selectivity in recruiting; (3) high wages; (4) incentive
pay; (5) employee ownership; (6) information sharing; (7) participation and empowerment; (8) teams and job redesign; (9) training and
skill development; (10) cross-utilization and cross-training; (11)
symbolic egalitarianism; (12) wage compression; (13) promotion
from within; (14) a long-term perspective; (15) the measurement of
practices; (16) an overarching philosophy.[50] What I wish to do is
show how these human resource management practices are supportive of Kantian meaningful work. They are also consistent with
earlier human resource theory. In 1981, William Ouchi published
his famous book *Theory Z*, in which he argued for an organizational
structure that departed radically from the traditional American hierarchical form of management in favor of a participative management
style that more clearly resembled traditional Japanese management
practices. Ouchi described 13 steps he thought were needed to go
from the hierarchical form of management, which he called Theory
A, to Theory Z. An examination of those steps would show a
considerable overlap with Pfeffer.[51]

Moving from organizational studies to the shop floor one can
look to the quality movement in the USA in the 1980s and 1990s

for a defense of management practices that have much in common with our account of meaningful work. As Jeffrey Pfeffer himself has said:

> The quality movement has legitimatized management practices that have been around a long time but have not generated a lot of support, perhaps because of the language. "Worker empowerment," "employee participation" or "participative management," "employee voice," "equity and fairness," "due process," "high commitment work practices," and similar terms often used in describing the employment relation somehow seemed to smack of coddling the work force. . . . The language of quality and the political support behind the quality movement overcome some of these problems at least to some degree.[52]

A moral requirement that firms provide meaningful work would have been considered impossibly utopian until recently. However, if US firms must be concerned with the quality of their products in order to survive in international competition, then the provision of meaningful work becomes a prudential strategy as well as a moral one. Meaningful work provisions are not utopian; they can even provide a competitive advantage.

Out of the Crisis by the late W. Edwards Deming is often considered the Bible of the quality movement. Deming's recipe for quality focuses on 14 points. Although Deming is noted for bringing statistical analysis to the quality movement, an examination of his 14 points shows clearly that his main concern is with the management of employees. His management philosophy is one that a Kantian could endorse. His 14 points include a provision for training on the job, for eliminating fear as a motivator, for eliminating barriers that "rob the hourly employee of his pride of workmanship," and for instituting programs of self-improvement.[53]

The competitive necessity for quality products and the meaningful work provisions that are required by a concern with quality have been recognized by the United States government. In response to the perception that foreign manufacturers were producing goods of much higher quality than those in the USA, the government established the Baldridge Awards for quality. It is interesting to note how many of the good-practice criteria refer not to the product itself but rather to how employees are managed. Even more interesting is the fact that these good management practices embody Kantian language that respects employee autonomy and responsibility. Emphasis is placed on the following factors:

> (a) management practices . . . such as teams or suggestion systems . . . the company uses to promote employee contributions . . . individually and in groups. (b) company actions to increase employee authority to act (empowerment), responsibility, and innovation . . . (c) key indicators . . . to evaluate the extent and effectiveness of involvement by all categories and types of employees . . . (d) trends and current levels of involvement by all categories of employees.[54]

Finally, let us consider some actual businesses that seem to endorse a Kantian notion of meaningful work. You do not find language in the business world that captures the pure Kantian spirit very often, but occasionally you do. In Pfeffer's terms few corporations have the appropriate overarching philosophy. Max DePree, CEO of Miller Furniture, captured the Kantian ideal when he described work as follows:

> For many of us who work there exists an exasperating discontinuity between how we see ourselves as persons and how we see ourselves as workers. We need to eliminate the sense of discontinuity and to restore a sense of coherence in our lives. . . . Work should be and can be productive and rewarding, meaningful and maturing, enriching and fulfilling, healing and joyful. Work is one of the great privileges. Work can even be poetic.
>
> What is it most of us really want from work? We would like to find the most effective, most productive, most rewarding way of working together. We would like to know that our work process uses all of the appropriate and pertinent resources: human, physical, and financial. We would like a work process and relationships that meet our personal needs for belonging, for contributing, for meaningful work, for the opportunity to make a commitment, for the opportunity to grow and be at least reasonably in control of our own destinies.[55]

Milliken and Company, a privately owned textile company with 14,000 employees, won the prestigious Baldridge Award in 1989. A booklet used in recruiting describes the company as follows:

In the process of arriving at new levels of quality, nothing supersedes the inner working of the human being. . . . There is emphasis on finding the best people for every career and on continuing education. . . . At Milliken, people are called Associates – not employees – implying the importance of each one as a contributor to our common objective. . . . All of this assumes a participatory management approach.[56]

But perhaps the statement of corporate philosophy that comes closest to the Kantian ideal is found in the way Hewlett-Packard expresses its philosophy toward its people. This passage is worth quoting at length:

Our People
Objective: To help HP people share in the company's success, which they make possible; to provide job security based on their performance, to recognize their individual achievements, and to insure the personal satisfaction that comes from a sense of accomplishment in their work. We are proud of the people we have in our organization, their performance, and their attitude toward their jobs and toward the company. The company has been built around the individual, the personal dignity of each, and the recognition of personal achievement. . . . The opportunity to share in the success of the company is evidenced by our above-average wage and salary level, our profit-sharing and stock purchase plans, and by other company benefits. In a growing company there are apt to be more opportunities for advancement than there are qualified people to fill them. This is true at Hewlett-Packard; opportunities are plentiful and it is up to the individual, through personal growth and development, to take advantage of them. We want people to enjoy their work at HP, and to be proud of their accomplishments. This means we must make sure that each person receives the recognition he or she needs and deserves. In the final analysis, people at all levels determine the character and strength of our company.[57]

Now that a general positive relationship between Pfeffer's research and other research in management theory has been established, let us return to Pfeffer's list to provide an explanation of those practices that might not be intuitively clear. This will enable us to show how these items contribute to meaningful work as we have defined it. Cross-utilization and cross-training (Principle 10) is a technique that allows employees to do many different jobs. Symbolic egalitarianism (Principle 11) refers to the elimination of symbols of status from the workplace. Wage compression (Principle 12) refers to a policy that reduces large differences in pay between the top officials in the corporation and other employees, as well as differences between individuals at roughly the same functional level. If wage compression were adopted horizontally, the VP for Finance would not earn a premium over the VP for Personnel as is now the case in most US companies. Finally, overarching philosophy (Principle 14) refers to management's commitment that these employment practices are a basic corporate value.

Although some of the items on this list have received general management attention, most of the items involve a sharp departure from current business practice. A comprehensive implementation of all the items would be quite revolutionary. Certainly, a number of the practices are contrary to what is accepted as successful management practice.

Yet most of the items on this list offer a means for management to provide meaningful work for employees. They emphasize the importance of employee autonomy and independence. They emphasize the importance of a good wage. They are consistent with the development of our rational capacities and they do not interfere with an employee's moral development. They treat employees with respect. In the remainder of this chapter and in the next, many of these practices will be further elaborated and shown to be consistent with what a Kantian would expect of a moral firm. Using Pfeffer's list of good practices for the management of people, the abstract notion that meaningful work is work that supports the worker in leading a moral – and thus an autonomous – rational life can be given some content.

What is now required is to show how the specific items on Pfeffer's list are connected to the specific conditions of a Kantian notion of meaningful work. Meaningful work is work that provides an adequate wage. Principles 1, 3, and 12 are means for providing an adequate wage. Principle 3 (high wages) is obvious as a means to this goal. Job security (Principle 1) has already been addressed in the first part of this chapter on the morality of downsizing. Much downsizing is wrong because it violates the negative freedom of employees. In addition, economic security is often what employees want most as an element of positive liberty. Job security is essential because it is necessary for achieving the characteristics of meaningful work. Thus, Kantian morality requires it.

Despite the fact that many firms behave immorally here – and some like those managed by Al Dunlop flaunt their immoral behavior – other companies try to provide employment security. For many years IBM was the leader in this regard, but bad economic times in the 1990s led to the abandonment of IBM's policy. One company that still provides security for employees is – as one would expect from reading the previous quotations – Hewlett-Packard. William Ouchi describes Hewlett-Packard's policy as follows:

> Twice in recent times, Hewlett-Packard has adopted the nine-day fortnight along with a hiring freeze, a travel freeze, and the elimination of perquisites. Each time these steps kept employees on while other companies in the industry had layoffs. The result at Hewlett-Packard has been the lowest voluntary turnover rate, the most experienced workforce in the industry, and one of the highest rates of growth and profitability.[58]

Wage compression would partly address a developing social problem. Many people find that despite the fact that they have full-time jobs, they are poor. In the last decade there has been a steady increase in the ratio of the salaries of the top officials in a firm to wages paid to the least well compensated member of the firm. Moreover, the living standards of those at the bottom, often referred to as the working poor, have declined. Wage compression would be something of a corrective here. A situation where the rich get richer while the working poor fail to achieve an adequate standard of living is not acceptable to a Kantian.

Another important component of meaningful work is autonomy and independence. Principle 2, participation and empowerment, speaks directly to that issue.

Autonomy and independence are aided by the fact that more and more companies are adopting a policy of flex time. Flex time gives employees greater latitude over their work schedules. Baldridge Award winners Ritz Carleton and Granite Rock are noted for their flex time programs.

We have already seen that participation is a requirement in

decisions regarding layoffs if the employment contract is not to be viewed as coercive. But participation is also required for positive freedom as well as for negative freedom. In the next chapter, where participation is discussed in much more detail, I show that participation is one of the key steps in the democratization of the firm.

Another requirement of meaningful work is that the work contribute to the development of the employees' rational capacities. Principles 2 (selectivity in recruiting), 6 (information sharing), 8 (teams and job redesign), 9 (training and skill development), 10 (cross-utilization and cross-training), and 13 (promotion from within) are all a means to this goal. By selecting the right people in the first place, you do not get people who are overqualified for the job. Working on a job for which you are overqualified is usually boring and frustrating because it does not make best use of your rational capacities. All the other items on the list contribute to skill development, which is both valuable in itself (recall that one of Kant's imperfect duties is the duty to develop one's talents) and adapts one for changes in the workplace so that the employee can remain gainfully employed. For example, Pfeffer argues for the importance of cross-utilization. Routine assembly line work is often work that is dull, boring, and repetitious. By training a worker to do many different jobs a firm can eliminate or greatly mitigate the drudgery of assembly line manufacturing. Cross-utilization makes teamwork possible and vice versa. In fact many of these principles fit together to transform traditional manufacturing work into an approach more compatible with a Kantian theory of meaningful work.

One principle, Principle 11 (symbolic egalitarianism) is also necessary for self-respect and is a condition of fairness. It breaks down some of the class barriers that say not only is the work that I do different from yours, but it is more valuable than yours, and thus I am a more valuable person. The person who is doing what is perceived to be inferior work thus loses self-respect – and loses it unjustly. A business firm is a cooperative enterprise and thus every task is valuable to the enterprise. Market conditions, and other legitimate factors, may justify the fact that we pay one job category more than another, but these conditions do not justify inequality of respect.

This point has been recognized by many firms. You can see from the emphasis on teams that work, for many, is a social activity and the achievement of meaningful work requires the appropriate support of the organization. In chapter 3 we shall look at meaningful work in its organizational context. Since an organization is composed of persons, the humanity of each person in an organization must be treated as an end. Chapter 3 will extend the Kantian moral philosophy to the business organization to determine how the humanity of the members of a business organization may be treated as an end. In doing so we shall examine and critically evaluate business structures to see the extent to which they either inhibit or support the possibility of meaningful work.

In summary of the analysis of this chapter, we have tried to apply to the business context the message of the second formulation of the categorical imperative to treat the humanity in a person as an end in itself and never as a means merely. To do that a firm must treat all its corporate stakeholders in a noncoercive and nondeceptive manner. We have illustrated that principle with respect to management's obligations to employees. We have also shown how treating employees as ends in themselves, in contrast to merely using them, requires an obligation on the part of management to provide meaningful work. Finally, we have tried to develop a normative framework of meaningful work consistent with Kantianism and tried to show how good management practice can be supportive of this Kantian vision of meaningful work. Thus, Kant's ethics can inspire business firms to feats more noble than merely making money.

Notes

1   Richard Parker has correctly pointed out that if the substitution of the machines made the jobs of the remaining workers more meaningful then Kant would not oppose the substitution of one for the other. After all, machines often replace the drudgery. However, my point is that Kant would oppose the substitution of machines for people just because the cost of machines went down relative to the costs of people.

2   Immanuel Kant, *Foundations of the Metaphysics of Morals* 1785, (New York: Macmillan, 1990), p. 46.

3   Ibid., p. 52.

4   Thomas E. Hill, Jr, *Dignity and Practical Reason in Kant's Moral Theory* (Ithaca, NY: Cornell University Press, 1992), pp. 36–7.

5   Kant, *Foundations*, p. 36.

6   I am indebted to Bryan Frances for this point.

7   Kant, *Foundations*, p. 64.

8   Immanuel Kant, *Critique of Practical Reason* 1788 (Upper Saddle River, NJ: Prentice Hall, 1993), pp. 33–4.

9   Onora O'Neill, *Constructions of Reason* (New York: Cambridge University Press, 1989), p. 53.

10 Christine M. Korsgaard, *Creating the Kingdom of Ends* (New York: Cambridge University Press, 1996), p. 167.

11 O'Neill, *Constructions of Reason*, pp. 57, 59.

12 Ibid., p. 113.

13 Korsgaard, *Creating the Kingdom of Ends*, pp. 140, 141.

14 Oliver Williamson, "Corporate Governance," *Yale Law Journal* 93 (1984), pp. 1,197–230.

15 R. Edward Freeman and William M. Evan, "Corporate Governance: A Stakeholder Interpretation," *The Journal of Behavioral Economics* 19 (1990), pp. 337–59. There is much more to the Freeman–Evan argument but it is too complex to be discussed here.

16 This example was provided by Deborah Johnson.

17 O'Neill, *Constructions of Reason*, pp. 122–3.

18 Denis Arnold, *Coercion and Moral Responsibility* (Ann Arbor, MI: UMI Dissertation Services, 1997), pp. 120–30.

19 Henningsen vs. Bloomfield Motors, Inc. and Chrysler Corporation, *Atlantic Reporter* 161 A2d.

20 John Case, *Open Book Management* (New York: HarperCollins Publishers, 1995), pp. 45, 46.

21 This example is taken from Francis Fukuyama's *Trust* (New York: Free Press, 1995), pp. 7–8.

22 Jennifer Reingold, "Executive Pay," *Business Week* April 21, 1997, pp. 58–66.

23 Ibid., pp. 59–60.

24 John Case, *Open Book Management*, pp. 108–9.

25 David Bollier, *Aiming Higher* (New York: American Management Association, 1996), p. 216.

26 Ibid., p. 218.

27 Dean Takahashi, "Hey Big Spender: Intel Shares Wealth With Its Employees," *Wall Street Journal* February 12, 1997, p. B6.

28 Ibid.

29 Douglas McGregor, *The Human Side of Enterprise* (New York: McGraw, 1960), p. 114.

30　Jeffrey Pfeffer, *Competitive Advantage Through People* (Boston: Harvard Business School Press, 1994), pp. 100–4.

31　Alan S. Blinder (ed.), *Paying for Productivity* (Washington, DC: Brookings Institute, 1990), p. 4.

32　David I. Levine and Laura D'Andrea Tyson, "Participation, Productivity, and the Firm's Environment," in Blinder, *Paying for Productivity*, p. 184.

33　Gerald Marwell and Ruth E. Ames, "Economists Free Ride, Does Anyone Else?" *Journal of Public Economics* 15 (1981), pp. 295–310.

34　Christopher Earley, "East Meets West Meets Mideast: Further Explorations of Collectivistic and Individualistic Work Groups," *Academy of Management Journal* 36 (1993), pp. 319–48.

35　Hill, *Dignity*, pp. 40–1.

36　Recall that an imperfect duty is one that you need to act upon on some occasions but not on all occasions. An imperfect duty should be distinguished from a perfect duty, which is a duty one must always act on whenever the duty is present. Thus, our duty not to lie is a perfect duty but our duty to aid others is imperfect.

37　Immanuel Kant, "Metaphysical Principles of Virtue," *The Metaphysics of Morals* (1797), in *Ethical Philosophy* 2nd edn (Indianapolis: Hackett Publishing, 1994), p. 43.

38　Ibid., p. 52.

39　Hill, *Dignity*, chapter 8.

40　O'Neill, *Constructions of Reason*, p. 114.

41　Ibid., p. 115.

42　Immanuel Kant, *Lectures on Ethics* 1775 (New York: Harper Torchbooks, 1963), pp. 160–1.

43　Ibid., pp. 177, 181, 185.

44　Although admittedly Kant wants a job to provide more than a living wage. A living wage is a necessary but not sufficient condition for a "good" job.

45　Ibid., p. 184.

46　Immanuel Kant, *Metaphysical Principles of Virtue* 1797, in *Ethical Philosophy*, p. 99.

47　Again, I am indebted to Bryan Frances for the formalization of this summary. The argument has been reformulated after Robert Frederick pointed out the earlier version's inadequacies.

48　Although business ethicists have not emphasized meaningful work, some are giving it attention. Joanne Cuilla and Al Gini have both made important contributions. My own thinking on this topic has evolved from discussions with my graduate student Kathryn Brewer.

49　I am not claiming that the only way one can gain autonomy and independence is through work that provides wages sufficient for independence. One can gain self-respect by being a priest or by being an impoverished artist. One can also gain self-respect by identifying with a group or cause. However, if work in corporations is chosen and is to be morally justified, then something like the arguments I have attributed to Kant are necessary. I am grateful to Tanya Kostova for raising this issue.

50 Pfeffer, *Competitive Advantage Through People*, chapter 2.

51 Ouchi's steps 2 and 3 involve developing a management philosophy. His steps 1, 7, 8, 11, and 12 all refer to the necessity for participation. Ouchi's step 8 refers to job security; his steps 5 and 10 address the need for training and skill development. Step 9 refers to a plan that enables the firm to retain and promote valued employees while at the same time permitting a more egalitarian pay structure. See William Ouchi, *Theory Z* (Reading, MA: Addison Wesley, 1981).

52 Pfeffer, *Competitive Advantage Through People*, pp. 215–16.

53 W. Edwards Deming, *Out of the Crisis* (Cambridge, MA: MIT Center for Advanced Engineering Study, 1982), pp. 23–4.

54 Quoted in Pfeffer, *Competitive Advantage Through People*, p. 209.

55 Max DePree, *Leadership Is An Art* (New York: Dell Publishing, 1989), pp. 23, 32.

56 Quoted in Pfeffer, *Competitive Advantage Through People*, p. 212.

57 Quoted in Ouchi, *Theory Z*, pp. 136–7.

58 Ibid., p. 118.

3

The Firm as a Moral Community

[Loyalty-based management] is about motivation and behavior, not marketing or finance or product development. And as we keep repeating, it is about customers, employees, and investors, all of whom are people. In the second place loyalty-based management is about people in a more abstract sense. It is about humanistic values and principles of the kind people devote their lives to, outside work and sometimes on the job as well. . . . Employees are proud that they and their colleagues treat customers and each other the way that they themselves would like to be treated. They see their work experience as more than a selfish, competitive game. (Frederick F. Reichheld)[1]

Introduction

Business leaders have discovered the virtues of cooperation. They realize that a successful business requires cooperation within the firm even as it competes with other firms. Business has garnered huge savings by eliminating layers of hierarchy. In so doing business leaders argue that they wish to empower employees further down the hierarchy. To accomplish this managers have discovered the virtues of teamwork. As a result, managers believe that their businesses will be more profitable.

Significantly, there are ethical reasons for making these changes as well and Kant's moral theory provides the justification. For Kant, any cooperative enterprise among people must contain a moral dimension. Since it is persons who are cooperating, persons have dignity and their humanity should be respected. Thus, organizations should not use people and should contribute to their development as rational moral persons. In that respect, organizations, including businesses, should be moral communities. In this chapter I use Kantian moral theory to provide the principles for a moral business firm. I begin by arguing that a Kantian views an organization in a certain way.

Viewing Organizations and Human Nature

A Kantian must reject a purely instrumental view of organizations. I believe this follows from Kant's notion of the kingdom of ends and his theory of respect for persons. The best quotation distinguishing an instrumental view of organizations from a moral view of organizations as a means for carrying out the shared purposes of persons is from John Rawls. What I am referring to is Rawls's concept of a social union in the last third of *A Theory of Justice*. Rawls argues as follows:

> Thus we are led to the notion of a private society. Its chief features are first that the persons comprising it, whether they are human individuals or associations, have their own private ends which are either competing or independent, but not in any case complementary. And second institutions are not to have any value in themselves, the activity of engaging in them not being counted as a good but if anything a burden. Thus each person assesses social arrangements solely as a means to private ends. . . . The social nature of mankind is best seen by contrast with the conception of private society. Thus human beings have in fact shared final ends and they value their common institutions and activities as goods in themselves. We need one another as partners in ways of life that are engaged in for their own sake and the successes and enjoyments of others are necessary for, and complementary to, our own good.[2]

Institutions that embodied these common activities and shared final ends were called social unions and the just society should be a social union of social unions. There does seem to be a great similarity between Kant's notion of the kingdom of ends and Rawls's concept of a social union, whatever the other differences in their philosophies. When an organization is viewed as an instrument for the achievement of one's own ends, then it appears that a person is simply using the organization, and thus using the people in the organization for their own ends. This would violate the second formulation of the categorical imperative. To avoid such a violation, the members of the organization would have to agree on the norms that are to govern the enterprise and their treatment of each other. But such an agreement transforms the organization into a sphere of cooperative activity – at least to a minimal extent. The association of persons is no longer simply a private society. In the context of the business enterprise part of what it means for a business to be a kingdom of ends is that it should be viewed as a social union, a moral community, or a kingdom of ends.

Most organizational theorists try to remain social scientists and describe how organizations are; they do not prescribe how organizations should be. One major exception to this view is Harvard Business School's Chris Argyris. Argyris's work is in the area referred to as personality and organization theory (P and O theory). The focus of this research is to show how organizational design affects human behavior, especially productive behavior in the workplace. However, Argyris argues that P and O research need not be limited to how people behave in extant business organizations. Rather,

> Man should be studied in terms of what he is capable of, not only, how he actually behaves. In the case of P and O theory, for example, the researcher could conduct research on worlds that would permit greater expression of the adult ends of the continua [autonomy, self-actualization, and a long-range time perspective].[3]

In business terms what might one of these alternative worlds look like? According to Argyris, one such world would be one "where trust, openness, and individuality are able to predominate."[4] In his 1964 classic *Integrating the Individual and the Organization*, Argyris is extremely sensitive to the charge that management theory is often suspect because those who use it wish to manipulate members of the organization. But he clearly sees the business organization as providing meaningful work in the sense defined in chapter 2. He says:

> Happiness, morale, and satisfaction are not going to be highly relevant guides in our discussion. Individual competence, commitment,

self-responsibility, fully functioning individuals and active, viable, vital organizations will be the kinds of criteria that we will keep foremost in our minds.[5]

Argyris's normative perspective is clearly consistent with constructing a Kantian kingdom of ends in the business world. We will have more to say about Argyris and his disciples' work later.

Over 35 years ago Douglas McGregor published a highly influential book entitled *The Human Side of Enterprise*.[6] The book contrasted "Theory X" with "Theory Y" forms of management. Theory X assumed that people had an inherent dislike of work and would avoid it if possible. Also, the average human being seeks to avoid responsibility.[7] Because most employees disliked much of their work, a highly directed management style was necessary to make them productive. The Theory X approach to human nature remains embedded in most of economics, including transaction cost economics and agency theory. Oliver Williamson's work assumes that people will behave opportunistically, which he defines as self-seeking with guile.[8] In agency theory, where one person (the agent) works for another (the principal) and where the principal cannot constantly monitor the agent, you have what is called an agency problem. This problem arises because agency theory assumes the agent will always act on her interest rather than for the interests of the principal.

Managers who have a Theory X view of human nature engage in a high level of monitoring, including surveillance. The Office of Technology Assessment estimates that in 1988, ten million American workers were subject to concealed video and computer monitoring. From 1985 to 1988 the number of surveillance systems sold to business firms tripled to 70,000.[9] Obviously, this kind of activity undermines trust between managers and employees. It also indicates great skepticism about the ability of people to behave morally.

Theory Y assumes the opposite: that employees prefer to be self-directed. They want to act imaginatively and creatively and are willing to assume responsibility. They also act morally much of the time and can be trusted. More specifically, McGregor named six assumptions behind Theory Y's view of human nature:

1. The expenditure of physical and mental effort in work is as natural as play or rest. The average human being does not inherently dislike

work. . . . 2. External control and the threat of punishment are not the only means for bringing about effort toward organizational objectives. Man will exercise self-direction and self-control in the service of objectives to which he is committed. 3. Commitment to objectives is a function of the rewards associated with their achievement. The most significant of such rewards, e.g., the satisfaction of ego and self-actualization needs, can be direct products of effort directed toward organizational objectives. 4. The average human being learns, under proper conditions, not only to accept but to seek responsibility. . . . 5. The capacity to exercise a relatively high degree of imagination, ingenuity, and creativity in the solution of organizational problems is widely, not narrowly, distributed in the population. 6. Under the conditions of modern industrial life, the intellectual potentialities of the average human being are only partially utilized.[10]

The Kantian adopts the Theory Y view of human nature. For Kant, if human beings do not behave as Theory Y would predict, their inclinations are interfering with their rational nature. That is, some desire or urge is preventing the person from acting in a rational manner. Or the person could be suffering from weakness of will. She knows what to do but fails to do it. Many people who have tried to stay on diets are personally acquainted with weakness of will. For McGregor, if human beings do not behave as Theory Y would predict, management or organizational incentives must have gotten in the way. Both McGregor and Kant would agree that the workplace should be managed so that the intellectual capacities of the average human being are fully utilized and that, so far as possible, work should require imagination, ingenuity, and creativity. All this contributes to meaningful work which is one way a firm can meet its imperfect obligation of beneficence.

It should be emphasized that my appeal to a Theory Y perspective is normative rather than descriptive. By that I mean that a Kantian would argue that a manager ought to adopt the Theory Y perspective. Now there certainly is good empirical evidence that managing from the Theory Y perspective can increase productivitiy and profitability in many situations, but there is also evidence that in other situations a Theory X perspective would be more productive and profitable.[11] A Kantian would reject the notion that the manager ought to adopt the Theory X perspective in situations where it can be shown to be more profitable. Some might argue that given the empirical evidence the Kantian is being utopian here. However, a Kantian could reject that charge by pointing out that management according to any theory of human nature results in a self-fulfilling prophecy.

What do I mean by a self-fulfilling prophecy? If people are treated as Theory X would predict, they will behave more like Theory X people. Conversely, if people are treated as Theory Y predicts, people will behave more like Theory Y people. Since a Kantian would contend that people should develop their positive capacities, both intellectual and moral, they should behave as Theory Y predicts. They ought to strive to be like Theory Y people. Now whether people behave like Theory Y or Theory X people depends in part on how they are treated. Since morality requires that people develop along the lines of Theory Y, then managers have a moral obligation to treat others as Theory Y predicts. In so treating them, they will tend to develop as Theory Y predicts, even if they have a tendency to be Theory X-type people. Kant would not permit anyone to treat others in ways that would make them less moral and less rational. Since that is what happens when people are treated as Theory X predicts, managers should not treat people in that way.

Creating the Kantian Moral Firm: The Kingdom of Ends Formulation of the Categorical Imperative

We now know that a Kantian should take a noninstrumental perspective on organizations and that the members of an organization should be treated from a Theory Y rather than from a Theory X perspective. But how should such a firm be organized and by what rules and principles? In other words, what would the business firm as a Kantian moral community look like? To help answer these questions we need to examine a third formulation of the categorical imperative.

The third formulation of the categorical imperative is sometimes called the Kingdom of Ends formulation. Loosely put, this formulation of the categorical imperative says that you should act as if you were a member of an ideal kingdom of ends in which you were both subject and sovereign at the same time.

What did Kant mean? Kant recognized that human beings

interacted with other human beings (ends). Thus, the arena of interactions was called "a kingdom of ends." A business organization, like any other organization, is composed of individual persons and since persons are moral creatures, the interactions of persons in an organization are constrained by the categorical imperative. This means that an organization, whatever its purpose, should be governed by morality. Because an organization is a community of persons, whatever else an organization is, it should be a moral community.

What are the laws which govern those interactions? Kant maintained that since those interactions were the interactions of human beings and not billiard balls, they should be governed by laws made by human beings. Thus, the laws should reflect the fact that the members of the organization are autonomous and rational in the practical sense. The laws that govern the interactions of persons should be self-legislated. Any self-legislated law for human beings must be capable of being universal in the sense described in chapter 1 and must treat the humanity of those with whom one interacts as an end and not as a means merely in the sense described in chapter 2. In an organizational setting this requirement means that any law (rule or principle) a person proposes to govern the interaction of the organizational members must be acceptable to all. Part of the task of this chapter is to spell out just what is required by the phrase "acceptable to all."

A first pass enables us to interpret that phrase as follows: When the rules that govern the organization are acceptable to all, everyone in the organization would be sovereign with respect to the law. However, since the laws that govern the interaction of the members of the organization apply to all persons, members of the organization are also subject to the law. Thus, an organization passes the formal tests of morality if the rules which govern the interactions of the members of the organization are consistent with the first two formulations of the categorical imperative and can be publicly advocated and accepted by all. As Kant said:

> For all rational beings stand under the law that each of them should treat himself and all others never merely as a means but in every case also as an end in himself. Thus there arises a systematic union of rational beings through common objective laws. This is a realm which may be called a realm of ends . . . because what these laws

have in view is just the relation of these beings to each other as ends and means.[12]

Whereas social scientists would look for the natural laws that govern those interactions (organizational behavior), moral philosophers would seek those norms that should govern such interactions. However, those moral norms include far more than the statements of the categorical imperative.

What Kant suggests is that we ask moral beings to act from laws that are publicly acceptable in the sense that they can be objective for every rational being. If the laws are publicly acceptable then one can be both sovereign and subject with respect to moral laws – subject because one is bound to obey them and sovereign because they are laws of one's own choosing. Let us apply this to business. Since all persons in economic affairs are moral agents, they are equal with respect to possessing dignity and intrinsic value. Thus, in a business firm organized as a moral community, the interests of every member of the community are equal to the interests of every other member. Our task in this chapter is to go from a purely formal analysis to some specific suggestions for management theory and organizational design. Borrowing from the title of a collection of essays by Christine Korsgaard, the task of this chapter is to show how managers should and could create the kingdom of ends within a business firm. This chapter will weave together insights from Kantian moral theory and some of the empirical work from organizational studies. Following Hill, I take the formula of the kingdom of ends to be a "heuristic model of the appropriate moral attitude to take when deliberating from basic moral values to moderately specific principles."[13] I then propose principles for the organization of a moral firm. These principles need to be consistent with the results in chapter 2, i.e., a firm should be managed so both the organizational rules and organizational structures are neither coercive nor deceptive and are supportive of meaningful work for employees. In other words, organizational rules and structures must support human freedom in both its positive and negative aspects as defined earlier. Finally, the organizational rules and structures must be fair to all corporate stakeholders.

As each of the principles for managing the moral firm are elaborated, I shall point out the implications of accepting these principles on organizational theory. For example, I shall argue that authoritarian hierarchical management forms cannot be justified on Kantian grounds; neither can Taylorism, nor the extreme division of labor. Rather, managing from a Kantian perspective morally requires some democratization of the workplace. I shall provide some suggestions from organizational studies and from actual business firms to show what a democratized moral firm might look like. By citing the experiences of successful business firms, I intend to deflect the charge that my account of the Kantian moral firm is hopelessly utopian.

The Principles of a Moral Firm

If one were to take the Kantian moral perspective, the following principles would be required for rule-making in the moral firm:

1   The firm should consider the interests of all the affected stakeholders in any decision it makes.
2   The firm should have those affected by the firm's rules and policies participate in the determination of those rules and policies before they are implemented.
3   It should not be the case that for all decisions, the interests of one stakeholder take priority.
4   When a situation arises where it appears that the humanity of one set of stakeholders must be sacrificed for the humanity of another set of stakeholders, that decision cannot be made on the grounds that there is a greater number of stakeholders in one group than in another.
5   No principle can be adopted which is inconsistent in the sense discussed in chapter 1, nor can it violate the humanity in the person of any stakeholder in the sense discussed in chapter 2.
6   Every profit-making firm has an imperfect duty of beneficence.
7   Each business firm must establish procedures designed to insure that relations among stakeholders are governed by rules of justice. These rules of justice are to be developed in accordance with principles 1–6 and must receive the

endorsement of all stakeholders. They must be principles that can be publicly accepted and thus be objective in a Kantian sense.

The principles defended

Principle 1 seems like a straightforward requirement for any moral theory that takes respect for persons seriously. One way to put this is to ask what it means to take the moral point of view. Most philosophers agree that the moral point of view involves at least a commitment to take into account the interests of those affected by our actions. I see no reason not to take the conventional interpretation here. Of course, the difficult task for morality is to decide how to act when the interests of various stakeholders conflict; that is, when providing for the interest of stakeholder x thwarts the interest of stakeholder y. What can Kantian moral philosophy say about the ethical means for resolving this conflict?

First, it should be noted that Kant would not require that there be one and only one answer here. That is why Kant's moral philosophy should not be seen as a system of moral rules to address all moral problems. All that is required is that whatever rule is adopted it cannot violate the categorical imperative in any of its formulations (Principle 5). However, any one of a number of rules for making the tradeoff might pass the tests of the categorical imperative. This result should be expected. As I argued in chapter 1, Kantian ethics is really quite permissive. In the words of Dunfee and Donaldson, there is considerable moral free space.[14]

But, second, if there is no one rule that necessarily would be rationally adopted by everyone, how can the rules which are adopted be universal? One might respond that this is the kind of question a manager should decide. But if the manager were to decide then the autonomy of stakeholders would be violated. Principle 4 prohibits a manager from taking a utilitarian perspective where the interests of some could be sacrificed for the greater benefits that others might enjoy.

Since autonomy is what makes humans worthy of respect, a commitment to Principle 2 is required and most scholars who apply Kant's philosophy to practical matters seem committed to it. For example, Edmund Pincoffs writes:

Participation is an instrument by which the valuation of persons as ends in themselves is expressed. It is as if the Kantian principles were determinable in any number of ways, but participation is one of the ways in which it becomes determinate. It does not follow that mere participation is of value (though it may have value) but rather follows that participation is morally valuable to the degree that it makes determinate the moral principle that we should never treat a man as a mere means.[15]

Thus, we have the justification for the second principle. All stakeholders affected by the rules must have some input into the decision-making process. The Rawlsian notion of shared ends and activities would require this as well. Thus, in the business context, all stakeholders should participate in making the rules that answer these types of questions. The issue still to be decided is how much and what kind of participation are necessary.

What is interesting is that empirical studies of participation designed to show the characteristics of participation point to many of those characteristics identified in chapter 2 as characteristics of meaningful work. For example, in one study by David Levine and Laura Tyson the following four characteristics of a firm's participatory human relations policy reflect this meaningful work perspective:

1   Some form of profit sharing or gain sharing.
2   Job security and long-term employment.
3   Measures to build group cohesiveness.
4   Guaranteed individual rights.[16]

Principle 3, which requires that the interest of one set of stakeholders cannot have priority for all decisions, provides a kind of organizational legitimacy. It insures that those involved in the firm receive some minimum benefits from being a part of it. After all, if one group of stakeholders were always to lose out whenever their interests conflicted with the interests of other stakeholders, the losing group would have no reason to continue to sacrifice for the common good. Those stakeholders would have no reason to be members of the moral community. You would not have a social union if the interests of one stakeholder group were always being frustrated. Obviously, activities that were always detrimental to one group would not represent shared ends and common activities.

In theory there are situations where the firm would be morally justified in violating Principle 3. Those situations would occur if one set of stakeholders always advanced rules or policies that violated morality. Suppose one group of stakeholders wanted to have all rules and policies discriminate against an ethnic group. Since discrimination violates both formulations of the categorical imperative, it is always wrong. If one set of stakeholders insists on discrimination with respect to every rule or policy proposed they should always lose. Although this situation is a theoretical possibility, I believe it is too remote as a practical matter to justify giving up Principle 3.

Principles 4 and 5 (the anti-utilitarian and the conformity to the categorical imperative principles) insure that the rules and operating procedures of the firm are constrained by considerations of Kantian morality. Principle 4 rules out utilitarianism as a criterion of decision-making in the moral firm. The reason Kant rejects utilitarianism is because persons have dignity which is beyond any price. Thus, the value of one person cannot be compared with that of another. In addition, the kingdom of ends formulation of the categorical imperative requires that the basic rules and practices that govern an organization must be acceptable to all. For these reasons in Kantian moral philosophy the numbers do not count.

The justification for Principle 6 (the beneficence principle) is based on an extension of the individual's imperfect obligation of beneficence which Kant defended in the *Metaphysics of Morals* and which we discussed in chapter 2. How do we get from individual obligations of beneficence to a firm obligation of beneficence? To avoid metaphysical issues concerning the existence of organizations independent of the members that make them up, let us appeal to conventionalism here. Both in ordinary language and in legal language we speak of firms having various rights and duties. Thus, Sears the firm has a right to have customers who have purchased Sears products on credit pay their bills. We also say that Sears the firm should not deceive its customers in its advertising. Thus, we have linguistic warrant for speaking of the rights and duties of firms.

What complicates this case is that some commentators, such as Milton Friedman, have argued that no firm has an obligation of beneficence because such beneficence would amount to stealing.[17] Corporate charity involves spending other people's money, i.e., the shareholders', for causes the shareholders have not approved. A full discussion of the strengths and weaknesses of Friedman's argument would require a book in itself. It should be noted, however, that Friedman's argument has sufficient credibility in the business community so that managers often feel required to justify corporate charity on the grounds that such charity contributes to the bottom line – a justification which causes great difficulties for a Kantian theory of the firm, as we shall see in chapter 4.

To counteract Friedman at this point, let us consider some arguments that could be given for a corporate obligation of beneficence. Two of the more common arguments are the arguments from citizenship and the argument from gratitude. The argument from citizenship extends the notion that individuals have obligations to support the state. Corporations are institutional members of society. Now surely if individual citizens have an obligation to improve society – to leave the world better than they found it – corporations have an even stronger obligation. Why? Corporations, unlike individuals, were created by society through charters of incorporation and thus are totally dependent on society for their existence. Society would not have created them unless they believed that corporations were in the public interest. As times have changed, society has increased its demands on corporations and one of the demands which has gained favor is that corporations contribute to the solution of social problems. Indeed, as I write this book President Clinton is leading a meeting of corporate executives and the heads of nonprofit organizations to make specific pledges to the solving of social problems. If the justification for corporations in the first place is that they contribute to the public good, why shouldn't corporations adapt to changing public perceptions of the public good?

The argument from gratitude has much in common with the argument from citizenship. This argument focuses on the benefits that society bestows on corporations in addition to their existence. Society protects corporations by providing the means for enforcing business contracts. Society also provides an infrastructure which allows the corporation to function and in many ways subsidizes corporations. Society provides an educated workforce with both the skills and attitudes required to perform well in a corporate setting. Roads, sanitation facilities, police, and fire protection are provided as well.

Of course, corporations do pay taxes for these services, but so do individual citizens and that fact does not exempt them from the obligations of citizenship and gratitude. In addition, corporations take advantage of the competition that exists among the various states to win tax breaks and other amenities associated with industrial parks provided by the state. Thus, an argument can be made that many corporations, unlike individuals, have not paid their fair share of taxes.

It should be noted that these arguments from citizenship and gratitude are consistent with Kant's argument for an obligation of beneficence. Kant's argument for the duty of beneficence is similar to that given for the obligation to help others in the *Foundations of the Metaphysics of Morals*. It is based on the fact that we need the love and help of others, so as a matter of consistency we have an obligation of beneficence to others.

> That beneficence is a duty results from the fact that since our self-love cannot be separated from our need to be loved by others (to obtain help from them in the case of need), we thereby make ourselves an end for others; . . . hence the happiness of others is an end which is at the same time a duty.[18]

What the arguments from citizenship and gratitude show is that the corporation has in fact received benefits from society, that the corporation needs those benefits, e.g., a state to enforce contracts, and more controversially that a corporation's tax payments do not adequately compensate for the benefits received. Thus, the obligation to assist society in return applies not only as a theoretical possibility but in fact. Although much more could be said here, I shall assume that these arguments provide sufficient plausibility for the adequacy of Principle 6.

Principle 7 is a procedural principle but it is also a very permissive principle. It basically says that if an organization follows the other six principles then it has complied with the requirements of justice. Thus, the seven principles function the same way as the categorical imperative functions for Kant. They provide a test that any morally adequate business institution must pass. However, there could be a number of corporate styles and practices that are consistent with the seven principles. The seven principles do not entail or dictate a particular corporate form.[19] I hope to show that in this way Kantian moral philosophy is demanding of business but not too demanding. Below, I shall show some of the organizational structures that are ruled out by the seven principles, but I shall also describe some enlightened organizational structures that are compatible with the seven principles.

Implications for Organizational Studies

A critique of authoritarian hierarchies

What relation does this abstract ethical theory regarding how moral firms ought to behave have to social scientific studies in organizational theory? Perhaps surprisingly, the fit is quite good. We begin our discussion with Principle 2, which requires that the moral firm get the participation of all those affected by rules and procedures before implementing them. Before beginning this discussion several introductory comments are in order. Although Kantian theory requires participation, there are many types of participation that might pass the Kantian test. In the course of our discussion several types of legitimate participation will be cited for illustrative purposes. My main task is to criticize those forms of management that are not sufficiently participative. Thus, the analysis is in the spirit of Kant, who seeks to show what actions or practices are impermissible. However, managers have considerable flexibility to choose among the various forms of participative management that pass the Kant test. The first management practice to come under scrutiny is authoritarian hierarchical management. Would Kant's requirement that management be participative require the abandonment of the traditional authoritarian hierarchical structure of management? I now argue that the answer to this question would probably be in the affirmative.[20]

The traditional form of business organization is hierarchical and authoritarian. Persons further down the hierarchical chain are given orders by those above them. They are expected to carry out those orders more or less without question. Organizational charts show reporting structures. The organizational charts of business firms are commonly reproduced at the end of case studies regarding these companies. Oliver Williamson has argued that hierarchical organizations promote efficiency and Williamson describes hierarchical organizational structure as follows:

> Joining an organization under the Authority Relation mode thus entails an agreement "that within some limits (defined both explicitly and implicitly by the terms of the employment contract) [the employee] will accept as premises of his behavior orders and instructions supplied to him by the organization." . . . The Authority Relation posits at the outset that a superior–subordinate relation will govern in both operating and strategic respects . . . a command hierarchy is a prominent feature of the Authority Relation.[21]

A Kantian would question the morality of a hierarchical structure that requires those lower down to carry out the orders of those above more or less without question, i.e., in a way that if the orders were not carried out you could be fired for insubordination. For an organization to respect the principle of humanity, the rules of the organization must rest on the consent of all the members of the organization. As Kant says, "Reason depends on this freedom for its very existence. For reason has no dictatorial authority, its verdict is always the agreement of free citizens, of whom each one must be permitted to express, without let or hindrance, his objections or even his veto."[22] What is sometimes forgotten in this age of the heroic or demonic CEO is that business is a cooperative enterprise. If an activity is genuinely cooperative, it seems reasonable to say that both the activity and the rules that govern it require the consent of all the participants. Consent is necessary in order to respect the autonomy of corporate stakeholders. As Korsgaard says about any cooperative activity, "Every rational being gets to reason out for herself, what she is to think, choose, or do. So if you need someone's contribution to your end, you must put the facts before her and ask for her contribution."[23]

Giving an order is not asking for someone's contribution. Thus, if hierarchical organizational structures entail the obedience of those lower in the hierarchy without opportunity to consent to the rules governing the activity, then hierarchical structures of that type do not pass the test of Kantian morality and should be abandoned. It should be noted that what is being criticized here is the tendency of hierarchical organizations to be authoritarian. Although hierarchies need not be authoritarian there is a tendency, as we saw in Williamson, for those in management and economics to assume that hierarchies are authoritarian.

Interestingly enough eliminating layers in the hierarchy, and thus layers of reporting relationships, is exactly what is happening in many business firms worldwide, although I admit that the motive for abandoning hierarchies is hardly Kantian.[24] Layers of management are expensive and are being eliminated to enhance the bottom line. Thus, the narrowing of the hierarchy is not being done out of moral duty. And, of course, a hierarchy with fewer layers but based on the assumption that those higher in the hierarchy give orders to those lower down is still authoritarian. Therefore most business firms remain authoritarian and in violation of Kantian morality.

Another critic of hierarchy from the organizational theory perspective is Chris Argyris, cited earlier. He has developed a continuum of human ends, with the more infantile at one end of the continuum and the more adult at the other. His psychological theory is that people develop from the infantile side of the continuum to the adult side. Specifically, this means that people develop from:

1   a state of passivity to an increasing state of activity;
2   dependence to independence;
3   behaving in relatively few ways to behaving in an array of different ways;
4   having shallow casual interests to having long-term interests;
5   having a short-term perspective to having a long-term perspective;
6   being in a subordinate position to being in an equal or superordinate position;
7   a lack of awareness of self to an awareness of self and a desire to have control over the self.[25]

Organizations, including business organizations, should adopt rules and have structures that support adult ends rather than infantile ends.

Argyris argues that in business organizations that have a hierarchical or pyramidal structure these adult characteristics are repressed and thus these management structures are deficient on normative grounds. For example, Argyris has marshalled considerable empirical support that shows that pyramidal organizations make workers dependent, submissive, and that these organizations constrain the possibilities for workers to use all of their abilities. The nearer the base of the pyramid you are, the greater the dependency and submissiveness.[26] In general:

> One can show empirically that the interpersonal world of most people in ongoing organizations is characterized by much more mistrust, conformity, and closedness than trust, individuality, and openness. This world, called Pattern A, can be shown to be consonant with, if not derivable from, the values about effective human behavior endemic in the pyramidal structure, or in what Simon calls the mechanisms of organizational influence.[27]

Argyris would agree with the conclusion that we should reject the pyramidal or hierarchical organizational form on moral grounds. Chapter 2 provided extensive arguments that an organization should support the autonomy of individuals and their ability to develop their human capacities, such as integrity, creativity, and excellence. Since traditional hierarchical structures do not support autonomy and self-actualization they ought to be rejected.

But how realistic is all this? Recall Williamson's argument for the efficiency of hierarchies. Interestingly, Argyris and other organizational behaviorists using psychological theory have provided evidence that counts against the efficiency hypothesis. Employees near the base of the pyramid adapt to their feelings of powerlessness in ways that undercut the efficiency of the organization. Slowdowns, absenteeism, noninvolvement, and withdrawal from work are just a few of the adaptive mechanisms.[28]

Research documenting the adverse effects of the hierarchical authoritarian organization stretches back over a 50-year period. Renis Likert of the University of Michigan distinguished four types of organizations: the exploitive authoritative; the benevolent authoritative; the consultative; and the participative group.[29] Since the participative group form of organization is the one that most closely represents an organization compatible with the principles of a Kantian moral firm, I shall only describe it. The participative group organization is highly democratic, with group involvement in setting the goals of the organization and in meeting them. Compensation plans are decided by group participation. Communication is initiated at all points in the organization and the flow of communication is multidirectional. There is a high level of teamwork in this type of organization.

Which of Likert's four types of organizations was most productive? Likert cited evidence to show the participative group form of organization was the most productive. Since this conclusion is not universally replicated, let us focus on some measures of productivity where the evidence is stronger. Participative group organizations have lower absenteeism, they produce less scrap, loss, and waste, there is more interaction among the members of the organization, and the information among members of the organization is more accurate.[30] Other things being equal it is obvious that an organization which has an advantage on these specific issues has an advantage in terms of overall productivity.

Thirty years later more recent empirical studies support Argyris and Likert, as we saw in chapter 2 when we considered the work of Jeffrey Pfeffer.[31] And for a particularly amusing account of negative assembly line adaptation at General Motors see Ben Hamper's *Rivethead*. Anyone reading that book will understand why General Motors has quality problems.[32] Thus, once again, Kantian ethics and sound management theory are congruent.

In light of this congruence why do so many managers still embrace authoritarian hierarchical structures? It is for ideological reasons, for reasons of managerial self-interest, especially the desire to maintain power, and because many adopt the self-defeating theory of human nature described earlier in this chapter. It is also because many managers are under the spell of the finance model of the firm. W. Edwards Deming has, until his recent death, been considered the guru of the quality movement, first in Japan, and eventually in his home country the USA. Deming, who pioneered in bringing statistics to bear on the problem of quality, nonetheless sounds like a humanist when commenting on the financial model of the firm. One of Deming's 14 points was the elimination of goals and quotas. He was opposed to Robert McNamara's philosophy of management by objectives. He also argued for the elimination of the annual rating or merit system. As one of his biographers has said of him:

> In Deming's view, the traditional financial mentality is the greatest impediment to quality management in the United States, because it often deflects attention from the long-term interests of a company's operations and because traditional financial and accounting measures offer managers few of the insights they need to plan for the future. In 1983 Deming addressed a group of students at Utah State University and tried to explain why numbers were of little use when it comes to satisfying customers. . . . What about the multiplying effects of a happy customer, in either manufacturing or in service? Is he in your figures? What about the multiplying effects of an unhappy customer? Is that in your figures? Did you learn that in your school of finance?[33]

The shortsightedness exhibited in attitudes to customers is also seen in regard to employees. An employee is seen as a cost. Cut the number of employees and you cut costs. If the argument works for machines, it works for humans. But as we saw in chapter 2, morally it should not work that way for employees. What Deming would remind the finance experts is that it does not work prudentially either.

Consent and worker participation

Other organizational theorists have followed Argyris and argued for an explicitly normative approach to organizational theory.[34] In 1988 Michael Keeley defended a social contract account of organizational legitimacy. Keeley's conclusions are in line with the requirement that a Kantian firm respect autonomy. For Keeley the key to the legitimacy of an organization is voluntariness (autonomy): "From a contractual perspective, the primary responsibility of those who manage organizations is to promote voluntary cooperation."[35] Since a social contract presumes consent, the social contract theorists are also supporters of a more democratic workplace.

But this emphasis on consent enables the defender of hierarchical management to respond to my critique as follows: Employees do consent to hierarchical structures when they sign an employment contract. They agree to take orders in return for a salary. Since this kind of argument was criticized in chapter 2, perhaps all that need be said here is that in the organizational context Kant would not permit a decision to abandon one's autonomy with respect to the rules and procedures that govern how one is to act. Kant specifically argues that we should not be servile.[36]

However, if hierarchical organization is morally illegitimate, what should replace authoritarian hierarchical organizations? The condition that managers get input from those affected by the rules of the business firm is a fairly weak condition. By itself it does not entail that managers should get input for every and all decisions. Moreover, getting input does imply a level of participation but it does not entail consent. An organization may get the opinion of a person regarding some proposed change without committing itself to getting the consent of the person. What does a Kantian theory of the firm require here? How far should the organization go in that direction?

It is the combination of Principle 2 – that a firm take the moral point of view – and Principle 4 – the anti–utilitarian principle – that requires an organization to respect the autonomy of its members. Certainly, a necessary condition of autonomy is consent. And it is this requirement that the autonomy of employees should be respected and that they should consent to the rules that govern them that morally dooms the hierarchical organization traditionally understood.

What I suggest is that Kantian moral philosophy requires a vast democratization of the workplace. A moral firm should be organized much more along democratic lines. As a minimum condition of democratization Kantian moral philosophy requires that each person in the organization be represented by the stakeholder group to which she belongs and that the various stakeholder groups must consent to the rules and policies that govern the organization. These stakeholder groups need to consent to the procedures for changing the rules. Ideally, democratization should go much further. Some hierarchical layers of management should be replaced by teams. Decisions made in teams should be consensual or at least be majoritarian. The persons in a Kantian moral firm would share the goals of the firm and thus the firm would be organized as a cooperative enterprise. Since the rules and procedures of the firm would have the approval of the various stakeholder groups, the firm would have the look of a representative democracy. To that extent at least the members of the firm would be both subject and sovereign with respect to the rules and procedures that govern them. Democracy at the team level would exemplify direct democracy and the ideal for team decisions would be unanimous consent. In terms of governance the Kantian firm would look very different from most firms today.

Traditionalists might scoff at moral demands for the democratization of the workplace. They would argue that such a scheme is utopian because the firm would be totally bogged down in the decision-making process. People would spend far too much of their time trying to reach a consensus and far too little time producing a product or service. However, I intend to argue that radical democratization is not utopian and I will make that argument both from management theory and from an appeal to actual cases of workplace democratization. Surprisingly, contemporary management theory has gone a long way toward Kant's goal.

At the theoretical level, the work of William Ouchi is instructive. In 1981 he published his book *Theory Z*, a modification of Theory Y management (discussed earlier) that Ouchi found embodied in many Japanese firms. The prudential lesson of Ouchi's book is that the key to Japanese success is how it manages people.[37] But as one examines the characteristics of Theory Z, there is a normative lesson as well. Theory Z management is consistent with the manager's obligation to provide meaningful work and with the principles of a moral firm, especially with Principles 2 and 4 that require respect for autonomy and consent by those affected by the rules of the organization. The essential ingredient is mutual respect. Ouchi puts it this way:

> Perhaps the most single notable characteristic among those who have succeeded at going from A to Z has been an almost palpable characteristic of integrity. . . . I mean an integrated response to problems, an integrated and consistent response to customers and employees, to superiors and subordinates, to problems in finance and manufacturing. A person of integrity treats secretaries and executives with equal respect and approaches subordinates with the same understanding and values that characterize his family relationships.[38]

Features of Theory Z include lifetime employment, individual evaluations that are infrequent and long term, nonspecialized career paths, a participative and collective approach to decision-making, self-direction rather than bureaucratic direction.[39] In his chapter on implementing Theory Z management, Ouchi begins by emphasizing the importance of honest and open discussion, including skepticism, as the first step toward building a Type Z corporate culture. In this way the autonomy of stakeholders is respected.

> In this initial process of reading and discussion, the substance of the ideas of Type Z organizations is important, but the process through which the discussion takes place is equally important. This process must reflect the egalitarianism, the openness, and the participativeness that are the ultimate objectives of the change.[40]

Ouchi points out that in Japanese firms everyone who is impacted by a decision has a role in making the decision. Where decisions involve locating a new plant or changing a production line as many as 60 to 80 people may be involved.[41] These characteristics of the process of becoming a Type Z organization are exactly the characteristics that Kantian moral theory requires.

Ouchi's work has been criticized on two basic grounds. First, some have argued that his work is not descriptive of Japanese management. Second, some have argued that he has ignored some of the ethical deficiencies of Japanese management. Specifically, some of the morally desirable characteristics of Theory Z management have been achieved by violating other ethical norms. For example, critics point out that lifetime employment is hardly universal in Japan. Many, if not most, women are shut out of the market and there is a huge cadre of part-time employees who have none of the benefits of lifetime employment. Most importantly there is nothing in a participative teamwork culture to prevent the group from doing the wrong thing and from creating an atmosphere of conformity such that even those who disagree go along. See, for instance, the Japanese novelist Shusako Endo, who described the participation of Japanese doctors in unethical medical experiments.[42] (Ouchi himself recognized some of these difficulties.)[43] Even if these criticisms of Ouchi are correct, his philosophy of Theory Z has something to tell us about autonomy and consent in the workplace.

So long as the characteristics of Theory Z are characteristics of respect for autonomy, Theory Z is in conformity with the Kantian requirement of participation even if the Japanese implementation of Theory Z is not.

Some researchers would have us look to Europe rather than Japan for examples of participative management. German law requires that labor have a place on the corporate board and more importantly managers are required regularly to meet with employees for purposes of dialogue and decision-making.[44] In the United Kingdom one of the longest and most comprehensive systems of participative management is found at Cadbury's.[45]

Another more recent example of participative management is dialogic action learning as developed in the later work of Argyris and Shon, Weick, and Nielsen.[46] The philosophical assumption behind this theory is that conflict, including ethical conflict, in an organization should be addressed through discussion and that to be effective that discussion must take a certain form. The key to success is the honest, open, and equal participation of all members in the organization. Richard Nielsen describes dialogic action learning as follows:

> Dialog as a form of action method is a conversation among leaders and others (peers, subordinates, superiors) about potential changes of means or ends behaviors. Dialogic method is both a way of knowing/learning and way of acting.[47]

There is no need to enter into an elaborate explanation of dialogic action learning, which has become very sophisticated. I introduce it here as one more example from organizational studies of the kind of research that is in process and that seems consistent with Kant's moral requirement that members of organizations have a right to participate in the formulation of the rules and policies that govern them.

Some of the most interesting recent research in organizational studies involves what researchers call "highly reliable organizations." Contrary to the accepted wisdom in management theory that urges managers to study organizational success stories, highly reliable organizations focus on their failures. They do so in order to be more reliable. What characteristics are necessary for highly reliable organizations? Answer: Many of the characteristics that would be required of a Kantian business firm organized as a moral community. Weick emphasizes the necessity for mutual respect.[48] Add to mutual respect, trust and trustworthiness.[49] But how is that mutual respect and trust obtained? By open and democratic discussion with special emphasis on obtaining diversity of points of view.[50] Since these highly reliable organizations exist in highly trying environments where the consequences of failure are immense one would expect these firms to be managed hierarchically rather than democratically. Despite the fact these organizations have many characteristics that are inconsistent with what one would demand of a Kantian firm, very Kantian notions of mutual respect, trust, and democratic discussion to elicit a variety of points of view are essential.

Although actual management practices have evolved in a direction that could be compatible with Theory Z, these practices regrettably are usually not in accord with what Kantian moral theory requires. These practices are introduced on efficiency grounds, not on grounds of morality. Were they not efficient they would not be introduced.

For example, with the elimination of layers of management, individual decision-making is being pushed down the organizational chain. Workers on the floor are given individual discretion and are being encouraged to make more decisions. So far so good. But although downsizing has sharply reduced the height of the pyramid, it has not eliminated it. Management practice has done much with teamwork at the bottom of the hierarchy. But they have done little to provide representative democracy with respect to the rules and procedures that govern the firm itself. Those decisions about rules and procedures are still usually made by senior management. Thus, many firms have tried to blend teamwork on the plant floor with a hierarchical approach to making and implementing the rules and procedures that govern the firm. Usually the result is failure. True democratization has not taken place.

But some firms are true believers and the democratization that has taken place in these firms is truly radical. Some even allow an individual a veto in certain group decisions. And if the notion of an individual veto seems silly, think of the Japanese and now often the American assembly line worker who is authorized to stop the line if quality problems are detected. A number of companies have gone some distance toward providing such autonomy.

A management philosophy committed to Kantian autonomy is found in a statement by Ralph Larsen of Johnson and Johnson (a firm which is on everyone's list of morally responsible companies). Larsen said, " I try to encourage, to give people a sense of self-worth and self-esteem, to instill confidence. I don't want people doing what I say: I want them to sort it out for themselves."[51]

One company that allows extensive workplace democracy is Levi Strauss.

> At Levi Strauss' jeans factory, when it was time to purchase new fork lift trucks, the drivers themselves got involved. They determined specifications, negotiated with suppliers, and made the final purchase decision, in the process saving the company money as well as obtaining equipment more appropriate for that plant.[52]

The airline with the greatest customer satisfaction is Singapore Airlines. Joseph Pillay, chairman in 1988, described his management style as follows:

> First we are above all a democratic organization. . . . We are not authoritarian, autocratic, or paternalistic. . . . There has to be delegation of authority down the line. . . . We endeavor to create an environment in which responsibility . . . can be exercised effectively at all levels.[53]

Some might argue that democratization of the workplace is all well and good for foreign firms or for firms, like Levi Strauss, that are not, for all practical purposes, publicly held; but democratization can't work in large functionally organized publicly held firms. However, democracy can be introduced one step at a time, in one plant, or for one major decision in one plant. A case in point is a Pratt and Whitney plant in Maine that was about to be closed because it was inefficient and had quality control problems. The new plant manager Robert Ponchak adopted a profit-sharing plan and extensive requirements for worker retraining – actions consistent with meaningful work as described in chapter 2 – but actions which were not introduced democratically. Not surprisingly there was worker resistance. When one of Ponchak's decisions regarding a new production scheme could not be implemented due to worker confusion, Ponchak embraced representative democracy. He appointed 22 representatives from both the factory floor and the clerical office to leave their regular jobs and to come up with a new pay and job classification scheme that linked pay to learning the new techniques. And they did and saved the plant from closure in the process.[54]

A critique of Taylorism

Another theoretical reason why traditional managers may oppose democratization of the workplace is that most managers endorse one of the hallmarks of the American business organization – the extreme specialization and division of labor. The intellectual mentor of this idea is of course Adam Smith:

> The greatest improvement in the productive powers of labor and the greater part of the skill, dexterity, and judgment with which it is everywhere directed or applied seem to have been the effects of the division of labor. . . . To take an example from a very trifling manufacture, but one in which the division of labor has been very often taken notice of, the trade of the pinmaker; a workman not educated to this business (which the division of labor has made a distinct trade) . . . could scarcely perhaps, with his utmost industry, make one pin in a day, and certainly could not make twenty. But in the way in which this business is now carried on, not only the whole work is a peculiar trade, but it is divided into a number of branches, of which the greater part are likewise peculiar trades. One man draws out the wire, another straightens it, a third cuts it, a fourth points it, a fifth grinds it at the top for receiving the head; to make the head requires two or three distinct operations; to put it on is a peculiar business, to whiten the pins is another, it is even a trade by itself to put them into the paper; and the important business of making a pin is, in this manner, divided into about eighteen distinct operations. . . . Each person . . . might be considered as making four thousand eight hundred pins in a day.[55]

Smith's insights were operationalized in American industry by Frederick Taylor and his followers. They have also been defended by Henry Mintzberg.[56]

However, such specialization and division of labor carries with it ethical difficulties. A workforce organized on Taylor's principles was not consistent with Kant's injunction that the humanity in a person be treated as an end and not merely as a means. If this is true, and there is evidence that it is true, then the extreme division of labor implied in Taylorism is inconsistent with Kantian morality and with Principle 5, above.

Although a revisionist account of Taylor is underway, the traditional interpretation of Taylor as expounded by Fukuyama clearly demonstrates why management according to Taylor's principles is morally inadequate.

> He tried to codify the "laws" of mass production by recommending a very high degree of specialization that deliberately avoided the need for individual assembly workers to demonstrate initiative, judgment, or even skill. Maintenance of the assembly line and its fine tuning was given to a separate maintenance department and the controlling intelligence behind the design itself was the province of white collar engineering. . . . The goal of scientific management was to structure the workplace in such a way that the only quality required of a worker was obedience. . . . A factory organized according to Taylorite principles broadcasts to its workers the message that they are not going to be trusted with significant responsibilities and that their duties will be laid out for them in a highly detailed and legalistic form.[57]

It should be clear from this quotation that Taylorism violates the worker's autonomy and that it creates a workplace that does not provide meaningful work; rather, it provides work that is deadeningly monotonous. Taylorism fails to treat the humanity in a person as an end rather than a means merely. It is also clear from this quotation that Taylorism is incompatible with the democratization of the workplace. Extreme specialization on the factory floor requires an authority who oversees the specialist to make sure that the specific parts come together in a product or service; extreme specialization among functions in the firm requires a CEO to make sure that the various functions mesh together to serve the purposes of the firm.

Interestingly, some of these moral difficulties were recognized by Smith himself. Indeed, Smith's moral condemnation of the results of the division of labor are far more stern than most contemporary writers. It is worth quoting his views at length:

> The man whose whole life is spent in performing a few simple operations, of which the effects are, perhaps, always the same, has no

occasion to exert his understanding, or to exercise his invention in finding out expedients for removing difficulties which never occur. He naturally loses, therefore, the habit of such exertion, and generally becomes as stupid and ignorant as it is possible for a human creature to become. The torpor of his mind renders him, not only incapable of relishing or bearing a part in any rational conversation, but of conceiving any generous, noble, or tender sentiment, and consequently of forming any just judgment concerning many even of the ordinary duties of private life. Of the great and extensive interests of his country he is altogether incapable of judging. . . . It corrupts even the activity of his body, and renders him incapable of exerting his strength with vigor and perseverance, in any other employment than that to which he has been bred. His dexterity at his own particular trade seems, in this manner, to be acquired at the expense of his intellectual, social, and martial virtues. But in every improved and civilized society this is the state into which the laboring poor, that is, the great body of people, must necessarily fall, unless government takes some pains to prevent it.[58]

This account of the Kantian moral firm from ethical theory may make sense ethically, but what about its chances as a practical reality? On that score I give you the candid comments of a Japanese competitor, Konosuke Matsushita, founder of the Matsushita Electric Industrial Company.

> "We will win and you will lose," he says. "You cannot do anything about it because your failure is an internal disease. Your companies are based on Taylor's principles. Worse, your heads are Taylorized, too. You firmly believe that sound management means executives on one side and workers on the other, on one side men who think and on the other men who can only work. For you, management is the art of smoothly transferring the executives' ideas to the workers' hands. . . . For us, management is the entire workforce's intellectual commitment at the service of the company."[59]

Thus, just as the hierarchical organization does not meet the Kantian test, so too does the extreme division of labor characterized by Taylorism prove a moral failure. Importantly, there are some managers and theoreticians who do not find that moral judgment utopian.

But what should replace Taylorism? Recently, and partly in

response to the success of Japanese capitalism, there has been an increased interest in teams. I want to argue that the team approach is more compatible with Kantian principles than Taylor's. To make this argument one needs to understand some of the structural characteristics of teams.

The cooperative workplace and teams

Teamwork requires cooperative nonopportunistic behavior. This is especially true where quality circles are replaced with problem-solving teams. Quality circles are more or less permanent teams designed to handle whatever workplace problems come up; problem-solving teams exist to resolve one problem. Thus, in a company with the problem-solving approach team membership will fluctuate radically depending on the problem. Therefore, the bonds of trust will have to be expanded. In a quality circle, the number of people the team needs to trust is quite small. In the problem-solving team the number is much larger; for all practical purposes trust should characterize all relationships. The firm should be a moral community.

However, the existence of teams to promote greater product quality and thus competitive effectiveness requires changes in organizational structure and rules. Deming recognized this early on. In her research on Deming, Andrea Gabor reports that the Ford executives who had hired Deming expected him to focus on the quantitative statistical methods he had developed to improve quality. Instead, what Deming wanted to know was how processes and people were managed at Ford. Gabor reports that Deming had been influenced by many of the theorists of human motivation discussed here, such as Frederick Herzberg, Abraham Maslow, and Douglas McGregor. Pffefer reports that Deming thought most people want to work, that they can take joy in their work, and that it is the moral obligation of management to create a system that enables workers to do so.[60] Deming also endorsed a more democratic workplace. He argued that most problems with quality resulted from problems with the management of systems and not the fault of the employees. He thought that employees were unfairly blamed for mistakes and were often the victims of mismanagement. Consistent with the position in chapter 2, some of Deming's 14 points for quality were admonitions to management to provide some of the features of meaningful work as it was defined in chapter 2.[61]

Obviously, teams undermine the strict division of labor extolled by Taylor. Since one of the motivations for teams is that responsibility for decision-making is passed down the corporate chain of command, then there is an increase in autonomy. An emphasis on teamwork is also inconsistent with traditional individualistic compensation plans. Deming also clearly recognized this point. One of the principles that underlay Deming's 14 points spoke directly to this issue:

> 6. Performance ratings that seek to measure the contribution of individual employees are usually destructive. Given a chance by management, the vast majority of employees will take pride in their work and strive for improvement. But performance ranking schemes can impede natural initiative. For one thing, by their very nature they create more "losers" than "winners" and thus batter morale. And since they don't take into account natural variation, they are inaccurate and unfair, and are perceived as such by employees. . . . The merit rating nourishes short-term performance, annihilates long-term planning, builds fear, demolishes teamwork, nourishes rivalry and politics. It leaves people bitter, crushed, bruised, battered, desolate, despondent, feeling inferior, some even depressed, unfit for work for weeks after receipt of rating, unable to comprehend why they are inferior.[62]

In summary, Principles 2 and 4 require that the workplace be extensively reorganized along democratic lines. To accomplish this, both hierarchical management and the extreme division of labor characteristic of Taylorism will have to be replaced by a system of representation at the firm level and by teams, both on the factory floor and across functional lines.

Organizational justice

Principle 7 addresses a different issue. It requires a notion of procedural justice for organizational relations. Procedural principles of justice are particularly important when employees are evaluated. Evaluations should be conducted in ways that respect the humanity of those evaluated. Empirical results in organizational studies have shown that persons whose performance is evaluated want to be evaluated in the way that Kantian moral theory says they ought to be evaluated. This branch of organizational theory is known as organizational justice theory. In the organizational justice literature, procedural justice refers to the perceived fairness of the policies and procedures used to make decisions. (Notice the similarity to Rawls, who defines justice as fairness.) William Ouchi has given a procedural justice interpretation to fair participative decision-making. Ouchi believes that the following is an accurate description of Western fair participative decision-making:

> The group can be said to have achieved a consensus when it finally agrees upon a single alternative and each member of the group can honestly say to each other member three things: 1. I believe that you understand my point of view. 2. I believe that I understand your point of view. 3. Whether or not I prefer this decision, I will support it, because it was arrived at in an open and fair manner.[63]

What people perceive as fair is consistent with how Kantian moral theory says people ought to be treated. Employees believe that work procedures are unfair if an employee is not treated with dignity and respect. Summarizing studies by a number of organizational justice theorists, Jerald Greenberg says, "It is reasonable to interpret all these findings as showing the same thing; namely that fairness demands treating others with civility and dignity."[64]

More specifically, G. S. Leventhal argued that procedures are fair if they meet several criteria: the extent to which they suppress bias, create consistent allocations, rely on accurate information, are correctable, represent the concerns of all recipients, and are based on prevailing moral and ethical standards.[65] Unfortunately, the number of studies testing Leventhal's concept are limited. However, it has been shown that judgments of procedural fairness are most importantly influenced by the interpersonal treatment people receive and the adequacy with which the procedures are explained.[66] Numerous studies have shown that there is a correlation between perceptions of fairness in performance evaluation and the opportunity to express opinions during the course of a review. Indeed, a refinement on the notion of input showed that employees wanted input prior to evaluation, two-way communication during the review, the ability to challenge the review, greater familiarity with the employee's work, and consistent application of standards.[67] A 1986 study by Bies showed that honesty, courtesy, timely feedback, and respect for rights were the most important factors in interpersonal treatment.[68] In a 1987 study Sheppard and Lewicki established the importance of "providing adequate information" and "assigning challenging and meaningful work" as components of perceived fairness.[69] One of the important findings in the organizational behavior literature is that people will accept bad results if they were responsible for the procedures that produced the results.[70] Although the language used by twentieth-century employees is somewhat different from that used by an eighteenth-century philosopher, the basic underlying ideas are the same. Persons want to be treated in business settings the way Kant says they ought to be treated. To that extent what people want coincides with what they ought to want.

This appeal to notions of procedural justice helps address an earlier issue discussed in this chapter. Since the needs and aspirations of the various corporate stakeholders are often in conflict, how are managers in the Kantian firm to resolve those conflicts? The first six principles for the management of a moral firm help here. The firm must introduce democratic procedures. Democracy does not eliminate conflict, but it can resolve conflict by providing a morally acceptable process for reaching decisions. Managers are rightly impatient with endless discussion when decisions are required. Norms of fairness in a democratic workplace provide both a practical and moral solution to issues of conflict.

Let us summarize the results of this chapter. I have shown that a Kantian ought to adopt a Theory Y view of human nature rather than a Theory X view. After explaining Kant's kingdom of ends formulation of the categorical imperative, I developed seven principles for a moral business firm. I then examined organizational structures to see what forms are inconsistent with the categorical imperative and the seven principles and which organizational forms are compatible with them. Authoritarian hierarchical structures and the extreme division of labor are incompatible with them. Stakeholder representation and teamwork are compatible with them.

In this chapter and in chapter 2 I have provided normative conclusions for the management of the typical business firm. However, I have also argued that management in accord with these normative principles is not utopian. A Kantian does something because it is right, not because it has good consequences, in this case contributes to the bottom line. Doesn't this discussion of bottom-line results undermine a Kantian theory of the firm? That issue is the focus of the next chapter.

Notes

Several of the ideas in this chapter are taken from my article "The Firm as a Moral Community," in Richard M. Coughlin (ed.) *Morality, Rationality, and Efficiency: New Perspectives on Socioeconomics* (Armonk, NY: M. E. Sharpe, 1991), pp. 169–83.

1   Frederick F. Reichheld, *The Loyalty Effect* (Boston: Harvard Business School Press, 1996), pp. 28, 29.
2   John Rawls, *A Theory of Justice* (Cambridge, MA: Harvard University Press, 1971), pp 421–3.
3   Chris Argyris, "Personality and Organization Theory Revisited," *Administrative Science Quarterly* 18 (1973), p. 160.
4   Ibid.
5   Chris Argyris, *Integrating the Individual and the Organization* (New York: John Wiley & Sons, 1964), p. 4.
6   Douglas McGregor, *The Human Side of Enterprise* (New York: McGraw Hill, 1960).
7   Ibid., pp. 33–5.
8   Oliver E. Williamson, *The Economic Institutions of Capitalism* (New York: Free Press, 1985), p. 47.
9   Julie Amparano Lopez, "When 'Big Brother' Watches, Workers Face Health Risks," *Wall Street Journal* October 5, 1990, C9.
10 McGregor, *The Human Side of Enterprise*, pp. 47–8.
11 References to this empirical literature can be found in Deborah Vidaver-Cohen, "Motivational Appeal in Normative Theories of Enterprise," *Business Ethics Quarterly* forthcoming.
12 Immanuel Kant, *Foundations of the Metaphysics of Morals* 1787 (Indianapolis: Bobbs Merrill, 1969).
13 Thomas E. Hill, Jr, *Dignity and Practical Reason in Kant's Moral Theory* (Ithaca, NY: Cornell University Press, 1992), p. 244.
14 Thomas W. Dunfee and Thomas Donaldson, "Toward a Unified Conception of Business Ethics: Integrative Social Contract Theory," *Academy of Management Review* 19 (1994).
15 Edmund L. Pincoffs, "Due Process, Fraternity, and a Kantian Injunction,"in J. Roland Pennock and John W. Chapman (eds) *Due*

Process, Nomos XVIII (New York: New York University Press, 1977), p. 179. I was alerted to this quotation by Joshua Margolis.

16 David I. Levine and Laura D'Andrea Tyson, "Participation, Productivity, and the Firm's Environment," in Alan S. Blinder (ed.) *Paying for Productivity* (Washington, DC: Brookings Institute, 1990), p. 205.

17 Milton Friedman, "The Social Responsibility of Business is to Increase its Profits," *New York Times Magazine* September 13, 1970, p. 33.

18 Kant, *The Metaphysical Principles of Virtue* 1797, in *Ethical Philosophy* (Indianapolis/Cambridge: Hackett Publishing, 1994), p. 52.

19 These formal principles will only work if those who have substantive ethical disagreements agree that a process solution is ethically superior to insisting on the moral correctness of one's position. As Bill Frederick has pointed out to me, it is unlikely that this will always be the case. Consider the opposing sides in the abortion debate. There is no willingness by some partisans in the debate to allow the issue to be settled on procedural grounds, e.g., by decisions of legislative or judicial bodies. At present I see no way to escape this difficulty.

20 If employees were to democratically decide to be governed by hierarchical management, then hierarchical management might be justified in those circumstances.

21 Williamson, *The Economic Institutions of Capitalism*, pp. 219, 222. Joshua Margolis indicated the relevance of Oliver Williamson to these issues.

22 Immanuel Kant, *The Critique of Pure Reason* 1781 (London: Macmillan, 1963), p. 593.

23 Christine M. Korsgaard, *Creating the Kingdom of Ends* (New York: Cambridge University Press, 1996), p. 142.

24 For example, see John A. Bryne, "The Horizontal Corporation," *Business Week* December 20, 1993, pp. 76–81.

25 Chris Argyris, *The Applicability of Organizational Sociology* (London: Cambridge University Press, 1972), pp. 108–9.

26 Argyris, *Integrating the Individual and the Organization*, chapter 3.

27 Ibid.

28 Ibid., chapter 4. It should be noted, however, that in this work Argyris is not totally opposed to the pyramidal structure. In chapter 9 he spells out the circumstances in which the pyramidal structure is efficient.

29 Renis Likert, *The Human Organization* (New York: McGraw-Hill, 1967).

30 Ibid.

31 See the summary provided by Jeffrey Pffefer, *Competitive Advantage Through People* (Boston: Harvard Business School Press, 1994).

32 Ben Hamper's book is not the only one that has criticized General Motors' insular, hierarchical, management by objectives approach. Other books include John Z. DeLorean, *On a Clear Day You Can See General Motors* (Gross Pointe, MI: Wright Enterprises, 1979). Many readers will also be familiar with the movie *Roger and Me*, a poignant attack on downsizing at General Motors and on the management style of Roger Smith.

33 Andrea Gabor, *The Man Who Discovered Quality* (New York: Times Books, Random House, 1990), pp. 7–8.

34 The most recent social contract approach is by Joseph Mahoney, Anne O Huff, and James B. Huff. See "Toward a New Social Contract Theory in Organizational Science," *Journal of Management Inquiry* 3 (June 1994), pp. 153–68. In their work they argue that the Hobbesian egoistic assumptions of traditional economic analysis must be replaced, or at least radically supplemented, by considerations of altruism, ethics, good will, moral sentiments, and trust.

From the philosophical side of business ethics mention should be made of two social contract theories. Edwin M. Hartman defends a Rawlsian-type social contract theory in his book *Organizational Ethics and the Good Life* (New York: Oxford University Press, 1996). Thomas Donaldson and Thomas W. Dunfee have defended a social contract theory that combines universal moral principle with a large moral free space where different moral principles might apply. They call their theory integrative social contract theory. See, for example, "Toward a Unified Conception of Business Ethics: Integrative Social Contract Theory," *Academy of Management Review* 19 (1994), pp. 252–84. Neither of these theories are Kantian and thus are not discussed further here.

35 Michael Keeley, *A Social Contract Theory of Organizations* (Notre Dame, IN: Notre Dame University Press), p. 19.

36 Kant, *The Metaphysical Principles of Virtue*, pp. 96–100.

37 William Ouchi, *Theory Z* (Reading, MA: Addison-Wesley, 1981), chapter 1.

38 Ibid., p. 101.

39 Ibid.

40 Ibid., p. 100.

41 Ibid., p. 44

42 Shusako Endo, *The Sea and Poison* (New York: Taplinger, 1972).

43 See, for example, Ouchi's discussion of the disadvantages of the Type Z organization in *Theory Z*, pp. 88–94.

44 Although union membership on the board is fine in theory, I do not wish to argue that it is sufficient for effective participation. I also admit that in practice the quality of union participation is less than desirable. A colleague has referred to union participation on the TWA board as "abominable."

45 See Richard Nielsen, *The Politics of Ethics* (New York: Oxford University Press, 1996), chapter 8.

46 See, for example, K. E. Weick, *The Social Psychology of Organizing* (New York: Random House, 1979); C. Argyris and D. A. Shon, *Theory in Practice: Increasing Professional Effectiveness* (San Francisco: Josey Bass, 1974); C. Argyris and D. A. Shon, "Reciprocal Integrity: Creating Conditions That Encourage Personal and Organizational Integrity," in S Shrivasta et al. (eds) *Executive Integrity* (San Francisco: Josey Bass, 1988), pp. 197–222; and Nielsen, *The Politics of Ethics*.

47 Nielsen, *The Politics of Ethics*, p. 94.

48 Karl E. Weick, "The Collapse of Sensemaking in Organizations:The Mann Gulch Disaster," *Administrative Science Quarterly* 38: (1993), pp. 628–52.

49 See Karl E. Weick and Karlene Roberts, "Collective Mind in Organizations: Heedful Interrelating on Flight Decks," *Administrative Science Quarterly* 38 (1993), pp. 357–81.

50 Kathleen M. Sutcliffe, "What Executives Notice: Accurate Perceptions in Top Management Teams," *Academy of Management Journal* 37 (1994), pp. 1360–78.

51 Thomas A. Stewart, "Why Leadership Matters," *Fortune* March 2, 1998, p. 82.

52 Ibid., p. 42.

53 Quoted in ibid., p. 112.

54 Joseph B. White, "Dodging Doom: How a Creaky Factory Got Off the Hit List, Won Respect at Last," *Wall Street Journal* December 26, 1996, pp. A1–2.

55 Adam Smith, *The Wealth of Nations* 1776 (Indianapolis: Bobbs Merrill, 1961), pp. 3–5.

56 Henry Mintzberg, *The Structuring of Organizations* (Englewood Cliffs, NJ: Prentice-Hall, 1979).

57 Francis Fukuyama, *Trust* (New York: Free Press, 1995)., pp. 225–6.

58 Adam Smith, *The Wealth of Nations*, ed. Edwin Cannan (Chicago: University of Chicago Press, 1976), part II, p. 303. For those using other editions, see book V, chapter 1, article 2d, "Of the Expense of the Institutions for the Education of Youth."

59 Quoted in Pfeffer, *Competitive Advantage Through People*, p. 253.

60 Ibid., p. 253.

61 Gabor, *The Man Who Discovered Quality*, pp. 5, 12–13.

62 Ibid., pp. 18–19, 253.

63 Ouchi, *Theory Z*, p. 43.

64 Jerald Greenberg, "Organizational Justice: Yesterday, Today, and Tomorrow," *Journal of Management* 16 : 2 (1990), p. 424.

65 G. S. Leventhal, "What Should Be Done With Equity Theory," in K. J. Gergen, S. M. Greenberg, and R. H. Willis (eds) *Social Exchange: Advances in Theory and Research* (New York: Plenum, 1980), pp. 27–55.

66 R. J. Bies and J. S. Moag, "Interactional Justice: Communication Criteria of Fairness," in R. J. Lewicki, B. H. Sheppard, and B. H. Bazerman (eds) *Research on Negotiation in Organizations* vol. 1 (Greenwich, CT: JAI Press, 1986), pp. 289–319; and T. R. Tyler and R. J. Bies, "Beyond Formal Procedures: The Interpersonal Context of Procedural Justice," in J Carroll (ed.) *Advances in Applied Social Psychology:Business Settings* (Hillsdale, NJ: Lawrence Earlbaum Associates, 1989), pp. 77–98.

67 Greenberg, "Organizational Justice," p. 406.

68 R. J. Bies, "Identifying Principles of Interactional Justice: The Case Of Corporate Recruiting," in a paper presented at the Academy of Management, Chicago, 1986.

69 B. H. Sheppard and R. J. Lewicki, "Toward General Principles of Managerial Fairness," *Social Justice Research* vol. 1 (1987), pp. 161–76.

70 Greenberg, "Organizational Justice," p. 410.

4

Acting from Duty: How Pure a Motive?

To say that profit is a means to other ends and is not an end in itself is not a semantic quibble, it is a serious moral point. (Charles Handy)[1]

Introduction

Every student of Kant knows that he insisted that we act from the proper motive; indeed, acting from the proper motive was *the* determinant of the morality of an action. As Kant put it:

Nothing in the world – indeed nothing even beyond the world – can possibly be conceived which could be called good without qualification except a good will. . . . Thus the first proposition of morality is that to have genuine moral worth, an action must be done from duty. An action done from duty does not have its moral worth in the purpose which is to be achieved through it but in the maxim whereby it is determined. Its moral value, therefore, does not depend upon the realization of an object of the action but merely on the principle of the volition by which the action is done irrespective of the objects of the faculty of desire.[2]

For several years now I have been arguing both in lectures and in published writings that moral conduct has a beneficial economic payoff. Indeed, when teaching executives or MBAs I begin by explaining Kant's moral philosophy and then provide a host of reasons to convince students that if a business firm practices Kantian morality it is possible to increase profits. Persons who know Kant have criticized me for not being faithful to Kant's central moral message: good acts must be done from moral motives if they are truly moral.[3] However, despite this approach and despite some of my language in this book, I insist that I have always tried to be faithful to the central Kantian point regarding the proper motive for moral behavior. Although I think guiding one's actions by Kantian ethics can in certain circumstances lead to profits, I think the primary motive for acting from the Kantian framework is that it is the right thing to do. I made this argument in a paper entitled "The Paradox of Profit" and repeated it in a paper entitled "New Directions in Social Responsibility."[4] In fact, I argued the Kantian line so successfully in these papers that Andrew Stark in his now infamous *Harvard Business Review* article used these passages to criticize me for being unrealistic and irrelevant to business.[5] Thus, I have been criticized for being unfaithful to Kant and for being a Kantian extremist. Some clarification is obviously in order.

Kant's Position on the Purity of Moral Motives

Let us consider a number of situations concerning the relation between profits and ethics so that some important distinctions can be made. First, suppose a business person can make a profit by committing an immoral act – breaking a contract, for example. Everyone would agree that such an action would be immoral. Nothing I have said should lead one to think that a Kantian could ever morally permit a firm's making a profit if in so doing the firm violated the categorical imperative. This would be true even if the survival of the firm were at stake. (However, a Kantian could permit a firm, on many occasions, to put profit ahead of an imperfect duty to aid others. See chapter 2 for that argument.)

Having made that point let us turn to one of Kant's few explicit business ethics examples. He says

that a dealer should not overcharge an inexperienced purchaser certainly accords with duty; and where there is much commerce the prudent merchant does not overcharge but keeps a fixed price for everyone in general, so that a child may buy from him just as well as everyone else may. Thus customers are honestly served, but this is not nearly enough for making us believe that the merchant has acted this way from duty and from principles of honesty; his own advantage required him to do it. He cannot, however, be assumed to have in addition an immediate inclination toward his buyers, causing him, as it were, out of love to give no one as far as price is concerned any advantage over another.[6]

This is one of Kant's most extreme passages, since he seems to be saying that since there is an advantage to being honest, the shopkeeper's honesty cannot be a moral act; indeed, Kant seems to be saying that the shopkeeper cannot be acting from the inclination of love. This passage seems fairly clear that when a shopkeeper can gain from being honest, then he cannot be honest in the moral sense. It may be that Kant has singled out the shopkeeper – and by implication, business relations – as being such that the moral motive cannot possibly be sufficient in these cases. If that is what Kant is saying then I think he is overstating his case. Nearly all of us, at least on occasion, have the experience of being motivated to do something because it is the right thing to do, even when that action will clearly be to our benefit as well. And most of us have had this experience early in life. The conscientious child who tells her father the truth because she is obligated to do so is acting from a moral motive, even though she would be punished if she did not do so and thus even though telling the truth is clearly in her interest. Indeed, this recognition that we should do something because it is right rather than because we may get punished if we do not is a sign that we are developing a moral sense.[7] What makes honesty in business relationships any more problematic than conscientiousness in telling your parents the truth even when you know you will be punished if you do not? If Kant does have this view of business he provides no argument for it. Indeed, in one other passage from *Lectures on Ethics* he seems to recognize this fact by introducing a notion of mediated goodness: "Thus honesty may possess a mediated goodness on grounds of prudence, as in commerce, where it is good as ready money."[8]

Thus, the fact that you have a prudential reason for doing something does not mean that it cannot be done out of duty – as Kant himself admits in *The Metaphysics of Morals*. The criminal law makes the commission of certain actions punishable by the state. That does not mean that a person who refrains from committing such actions cannot be doing so out of duty.

> It is not a duty of virtue to keep one's promise, but a duty of justice, one that we can be coerced to perform. Nevertheless, it is a virtuous action (proof of virtue) to do so where no coercion is to be feared. Jurisprudence and ethics [Rechtslehre and Tudendlehre] are distinguished, therefore, not so much by their differing duties as by the difference in the legislation that combines one or the other incentive with the law. . . . To be sure, Ethics also has duties peculiar to itself (for example, duties to oneself); but it also has duties in common with justice, though the manner of being bound to such duties differs.[9]

Kant is on record as saying that it is difficult to determine the actual motivation of people and thus even actions that appear as if they were done out of duty, may not have been. I agree that motives are notoriously difficult to determine, even when Holmes's aphorism that "even a dog knows the difference between being kicked and being tripped over" is taken into account.[10] Kant said:

> It is indeed sometimes the case that after the keenest self-examination we can find nothing except the moral ground of duty that could have been strong enough to move us to this or that good action and to such great sacrifice. But there cannot with certainty be at all inferred from this that some secret impulse of self-love, merely appearing as the idea of duty, was not the actual determinate cause of the will. We like to flatter ourselves with the false claim to a more noble motive, but in fact we can never, even by the strictest examination, completely plumb the depths of the secret incentives for our actions.[11]

Where there is a clear advantage to acting as morality requires, there is a tendency to think that duty was not the motivation for the action. But that still leaves open the possibility that the action could have been done out of duty – a possibility which, if admitted, is sufficient for my purposes. If Kant admits that possibility is open with respect to refraining from actions that could cause the perpetrator to be punished, that possibility should be open in business (as with the shopkeeper) as well.

Notice that I have not tried to argue that the shopkeeper could have been motivated by an inclination to benevolence (love), because even if that argument succeeded it would not prove enough. Actions done from inclination – including an inclination to benevolence – are not genuine moral actions for Kant. Thus, actions performed by good-hearted people, people who are naturally kind or sympathetic, were not considered by Kant to be moral actions (though he thought that it was good that such actions were done and the actions certainly were not immoral). Kant reasoned that actions motivated by inclination were not universal and thus could not be counted on as a ground for doing the right thing. Many people would not respond sympathetically to people who are in hospital and visit them. More importantly, an inclination cannot function as a reason for Kant. People who always respond sympathetically might respond that way when they should not. Thus, for Kant, only actions done from respect for the moral law (the categorical imperative) were genuinely moral. A visit to a sick friend was only a genuine moral act if the visit was motivated by respect for the categorical imperative.

> To be kind where one can is a duty, and there are, moreover, many
> persons so sympathetically constituted that without any motive of
> vanity or selfishness they find an inner satisfaction in spreading joy
> and rejoice in the contentment of others which they have made
> possible. But I say that, however dutiful and however amiable it may
> be, that kind of action has no true moral worth.[12]

What can we conclude from this discussion? For Kant, an action has true moral worth only if it is done out of duty. Actions done for reasons of prudence or even actions done out of the goodness of one's heart are not genuine moral actions. However, the fact that an action is prudent does not necessarily mean that the action could not be done for the sake of duty, i.e., done because it is right to do so.

Overdetermined actions

But what if an action is the result of two motives, performed not only because of a fear of punishment but also because it was the right thing to do (out of duty)? Some actions are performed from multiple motives. An action is overdetermined when there is more than one motive influencing the doing of it. Thus, if a business person does not cheat a child because she believes it is wrong and because she wants a reputation as an honest business person, then the action is overdetermined. What does Kant say about actions that are overdetermined? Would such an action be one that has genuine moral worth? There are several possibilities here.

If Kant is interpreted as a purist here, the only motive that would make the action truly moral is the motive provided by the good will, i.e., doing it because it is right. The fact that the action would also contribute to profit or avoid punishment cannot enter into one's motivation at all. Thus, the mere presence of a second motive disqualifies the action as good. If that is the case, it looks as if business people do few actions out of duty even if many of their actions conform to duty. Profits are almost always a consideration in a business decision. Should a Kantian in business ethics simply accept that conclusion?

Not if Kant is less of a purist than some have thought. Some recent commentators interpret Kant in a way that makes him seem less of a purist after all. Consider three possibilities for making the shopkeeper's action overdetermined:

(a)   The shopkeeper would not cheat the child even if she could get away with it. Thus, the moral motive would have been a sufficient motive in this case.

(b)   The shopkeeper would not cheat the child only if she thought cheating him would harm her reputation. In this case the prudent motive is necessary for the commission of the good action.

(c)   Neither the moral motive nor the prudential motive are sufficient for not cheating the child. Each is necessary and they are jointly sufficient.

What would Kant say about these cases? Clearly, an action performed on the basis of the motive described in (b) would not be a moral action. I know of no commentator on Kant who claims it would. I also think it is fairly clear that Kant would reject the action as motivated in (c) as a moral action. Again, I am unaware of any commentator on Kant who would argue differently.

That leaves (a). Kant certainly seems to recognize that situations like (a) exist. Indeed, the *Metaphysics of Morals* is divided into two parts, the "Metaphysical Principles of Justice" and the "Metaphysical Principles of Virtue." The principles of justice are backed by the coercive power of the state, while the metaphysical principles of virtue are not. As we mentioned earlier, an agent can have as her motive for acting on a principle of justice either fear of the penalty or the fact that it is just. What if a person is motivated by both considerations?

If the duty not to lie is honored both because there is a penalty for lying and because telling the truth is the right thing to do, is the action genuinely moral? Or, for it to be genuinely moral, must the fact that there is a penalty for lying be absent from one's conscious- ness? Richard Henson has argued that Kant could argue that (a) is a moral action.[13] For Henson, all that is required is that the motive of duty would be sufficient for the action if the other influences were not present. But Henson's way of handling (a)-like cases is not sufficiently Kantian for Barbara Herman.[14] She points out that there is an ambiguity in the use of "sufficient." It could mean sufficient if other influences were not present, or it could mean sufficient even when the other influences are present. Herman insists that Kant would take "sufficient" in the latter interpretation. Thus, Herman would insist that there are incentives for actions and reasons for actions: (a) would be a moral action for Kant if morality provided the reason for doing it, even if that reason coexisted with a non-moral incentive for doing it.

> When an action has moral worth, nonmoral *incentives* may be present, but they may not be the agent's motives in acting. If the agent acts from a motive of duty, he acts because he takes the fact that the action is morally required to be the ground of choice.[15]

On this account, if the shopkeeper were honest because it was morally required even if there was a prudential incentive in terms of a good reputation for being honest, the action would be a genuine moral action on Kantian grounds.[16] Actions which result in a profit for business can nonetheless be moral if duty was the motive guiding them.

Although I think philosophically this is correct, problems remain. The chief problem is that business people seldom describe their

putatively good actions in a way that would meet Kantian requirements, even when Kant is interpreted the way Herman interprets
him. Specifically, they argue that profit really is one of the reasons
for their action. Business people are more inclined to treat the
honest shopkeeper example as a (c)-case rather than an (a)-case.

Before addressing this difficulty it should be pointed out that
some business executives really do talk like Kantians here. A standard case in many business ethics courses is the Merck Company.
Merck discovered the cure for river blindness, a disease caused by a
parasitic worm carried by black flies that live along rivers in remote
portions of Africa and South America. The Merck miracle drug
Mectazin was specific to this disease and had no other uses, but
those who had river blindness could not afford it. Merck went ahead
and developed the drug anyway at the cost of millions of dollars. It
had hoped that foundations or the US government would pay for
the drug. So far Merck's motives seem not sufficiently Kantian. But
when no one would step forward, Merck agreed to supply the drug.
Then it realized there was no easy way to distribute the drug, since
those who needed it lived far away from highways or airports.
Merck then agreed to produce the drug and distribute it for free
forever. In making that commitment they seemed to meet the
Kantian demand. Merck ultimately made the commitment because
it was right.

The Honeywell Corporation provides a second example. James
Renier, former CEO of Honeywell has said:

> If we help people develop into the best they can become, and if we
> enable people to make their maximum contribution on the job, we
> will get the innovation and productivity we need. But I suggest to
> you that even if I did not get more productivity or make the
> company more secure, or improve profits, it would still be worth
> doing. It would be worth doing simply because it is the right thing
> to do.... Think of it [participation] as an ethical undertaking.
> That will insure that programs like ... quality work life help our
> people achieve their objectives and do not degenerate to mere
> manipulation.[17]

It looks as if these actions by Merck and Honeywell pass the
Kantian motivational test. By the end, profit does not even seem to
be an incentive for Merck. And Honeywell seems to be a genuine

example of a type (a) case as interpreted by Herman. With Honeywell, profit was an incentive but it was not the motive. The reason why Honeywell acted as it did was because so acting was the right thing to do. Moreover, Honeywell would have acted for that reason whether the incentive was present or not.

Strategic Payoffs and Moral Motives

However, since most CEOs do not think like Jim Renier, what are we to conclude about the morality of business actions that are simply in conformity with duty? Here I am referring to actions that are consistent with morality but are not done for moral motives; rather, they are motivated by a desire to enhance profits or market share. I have in mind companies like American Express that will donate to charity each time a consumer uses her American Express credit card.

One approach would be to argue that more CEOs should think like Renier. If one were to take this line, one would be making an argument that business people change the motives on which they act: do it because it is right not because it will lead to greater profits. In fact there is considerable evidence that both management scholars and other people speak like the most pure Kantians when evaluating corporate conduct. In other words, if people think that business is doing good deeds for the money, many people react cynically and discount the good deeds. A few people may even think less of a company that does good deeds for the money than it does of a company that simply does business (just produces a product or service the public demands.) For example, Milton Friedman says,

> Of course, in practice, the doctrine of social responsibility is frequently a cloak for actions that are justified on other grounds rather than a reason for those actions. To illustrate, it may be in the long-run interest of a corporation that is a major employer in a small community to devote resources to providing amenities to that community or to improving its government. That may make it easier to attract desirable employees, it may reduce the wage bill or lessen losses from pilferage or sabotage or have other worthwhile effects. . . . In the present climate of opinion . . . this is one way for a corporation to generate goodwill as a by-product of expenditures

that are entirely justified in its own self-interest. . . . At the same time, I can express admiration for those individual proprietors or owners of closely held corporations or stockholders of more broadly held corporations who disdain such tactics as approaching fraud.[18]

Or consider Albert Carr, who wrote the highly publicized and highly controversial *Harvard Business Review* piece, "Is Business Bluffing Ethical?"

> The illusion that business can afford to be guided by ethics as conceived in private life is often fostered by speeches and articles containing such phrases as "It pays to be ethical" or "Sound ethics is good business." Actually this is not an ethical position at all; it is self-serving calculation in disguise. The speaker is really saying that in the long run a company can make more money if it does not antagonize competitors, suppliers, employees, and customers by squeezing them too hard. That is true but it has nothing to do with ethics.[19]

Given the fact that people tend to agree with Friedman and Carr when they evaluate the motives behind so called "corporate good deeds," perhaps business people should take the proposed reform seriously. With respect to actions required by the categorical imperative, the fact that the categorical imperative requires or forbids them should be sufficient for the doing or the not doing of them. With respect to good deeds that are sometimes required by imperfect duties, then on those occasions where they are required, the fact that they are required should be sufficient as a motive for doing them. Thus, in business the fact that something is right in the sense stipulated should be sufficient for doing it. So long as that condition is met, following Herman and others, the inclination to seek a profit may also be present. But isn't such advice purely utopian? Could a business in a competitive system survive that way?

Interestingly, there is theoretical support to show that being motivated in such a way is not utopian, although it is somewhat paradoxical. Some business firms in some situations may be able to increase profits or increase their market share only if they act from the motive of duty. In his book *Passions Within Reason* Robert Frank provides a series of arguments for the strategic advantages that come with pure altruism. Frank distinguishes between reciprocal altruism and hardcore altruism. You have a case of reciprocal altruism when you do something good for someone in the expectation that they will do something good for you. For Frank, reciprocal altruism is not true altruism. Kant would agree. Hardcore altruism, on the other hand, occurs when someone sacrifices an interest of hers in the interest of someone else and there is *no* possible gain for herself as a result. Hardcore altruists are committed; their acts of hardcore altruism are done because they are right.

However, even though some actions are done because they are right, they may have a strategic payoff. Of special interest to business people is Frank's analysis of trust. Managers have discovered trust and have found that trust contributes to profitability by allowing an individual or a firm to engage in transactions not open – or not open to the same extent – to people who are not trustworthy. Partnership in a joint venture, or the ability to get venture capital, are standard business examples. However, partners or venture capitalists will only trust their potential partners if they believe their partners are genuinely trustworthy and are not simply adopting a trusting posture as a matter of strategy. Frank puts the matter this way:

> The honest individual in the commitment model is someone who values trustworthiness for its own sake. That he might receive a material payoff for such behavior is completely beyond his concern. And it is precisely because he has this attitude that he can be trusted in situations where his behavior cannot be monitored. . . . But even if the world were to end at midnight, thus eliminating all possibility of penalty for detection, the genuinely trustworthy person would not be motivated to cheat.[20]

It is important that I should not be misunderstood here. I am not urging that business people act from the motive of duty because there can be a payoff for doing so. Business people should do the right thing because it is right. On this point Frank is in complete agreement with Kant. Frank says:

> For the model to work, satisfaction from doing the right thing must not be premised on the fact that material gain may later follow; rather it must be *intrinsic* to the act itself. Otherwise a person will lack the necessary motivation to make self-sacrificing choices, and once others sense that, material gains will not in fact follow. Under the commit-

ment model, moral sentiments do not lead to material advantage unless they are heartfelt.[21]

I think it is fairly easy to apply Frank's point specifically to business. Frank is saying that if you act from duty you will be rewarded, but you must not think about or expect the reward because if you do you won't receive the reward. I want typical cases that will show that Frank is right in arguing that in business moral motives should be sufficient for action and that only if business people are so motivated will they reap the full advantages of morality. Thus, there are occasions when you can be profitable only if you are genuinely moral in the purest Kantian sense as interpreted in the first part of this chapter.

My first example is based on the foolishness of much advice given to MBAs in business school. MBAs are often told that every business decision should be justified on grounds of self-interest of the firm. Every decision should be motivated by the desire to make a profit. But business people look foolish when they say they are motivated by profit to do things that it is nearly impossible to construe as motivated in that way. Indeed, Kant believed that nonphilosophers support his view that a person would look foolish if she tried to explain a moral action on prudential grounds. In more contemporary philosophical language, if you ask about the morality of a person or action, and receive in reply a defense of someone's prudence, the respondee will have made a category mistake. A lengthy quotation from Kant is instructive here.

> Or suppose someone recommends to you as steward a man to whom you could blindly trust your affairs and, in order to inspire you with confidence, further extols him as a prudent man who has a masterly understanding of his own interest and is so indefatigably active that he misses no opportunity to further it; lest you should be afraid of finding a vulgar selfishness in him, he praises the good taste with which he lives, not seeking his pleasure in making money or in coarse wantonness, but in the increase of his knowledge, in constructive conversation with a select circle, and even in relieving the needy. But he adds, he is not particular as to the means (which, of course, derive their value only from the end), being as willing to use another's money or property as his own, provided only that he knows he can do so safely and without discovery. You would believe

that the person making such a recommendation would be mocking you or would have lost his mind.[22]

But strangely this is precisely how many management professors would have managers behave in business. They recommend managers to adopt practices that we have shown are consistent with Kantian morality and that most people would consider to be morally good actions — such as the use of teams or quality circles, or that workers be empowered, or that the workplace be organized more democratically — because these morally good practices will likely raise the profits of the stockholders. Wouldn't it be more sensible to adopt these management practices because they are right? Indeed, managers instinctively know this because they seldom tell the workers they are instituting these practices because they will lead to profits. If the managers truthfully announced that they were doing these good things in order to increase profits, how would an employee or customer respond? Wouldn't the managers be mocked rather than praised? So in dealing with employees, managers use the language of ethics and in dealing with Wall Street, managers use the language of self-interest. Of course, workers know that managers use the language of self-interest on Wall Street and thus they do not believe managers when they say that they are instituting enlightened business practices because it is right. As a result, unions block or inhibit such practices, or in the absence of unions the expected gains for these enlightened practices are not achieved.

These considerations led me to formulate an argument from "The Paradox of Profit" that went like this. Philosophers are familiar with the hedonic paradox: "The more you consciously seek happiness the less likely you are to find it." If you do not believe this, just get up some morning and resolve that everything you do will be done in order to achieve happiness. You will soon be miserable. Happiness is something you achieve, but not something you strive for. Happiness is the result of successful achievements, but is not itself something you try to achieve. For Aristotle, self-realization is what you try to achieve and happiness is the result of achieving it. It seems to me that at least to some extent profits are like that. If your focus on them is excessive, the less likely you are to achieve them. The conventional wisdom argues that business managers should focus solely on the bottom line. A Kantian thinks that advice is mistaken. Instead, the business manager should focus less on profit and focus more on doing the right thing, which in the context of this book means treating the humanity of all corporate stakeholders as an end and managing in accord with the principles of the moral firm. If managers manage in that way and do it from the motive of duty, profits are likely to result. (Of course, that will not always be the case; the manager needs to use her accounting. finance, and other business skills and needs to have good luck besides.)

A further consideration in favor of this point is a thought experiment I presented in my response to Andrew Stark in the Society for Business Ethics newsletter of February 1994. Your spouse wants you to attend an event you prefer to skip. You can (a) not go; (b) go in the hope that your spouse will go to an event you want to attend but that the spouse would rather skip; (c) go out of love. Which motive builds the stronger relationship? Answer: (c). Also, if you act out of (c) you are likely to get (b) results. But if the motive for your action is (b), you are less likely to get (b) results.

For a while I thought I was one of the few people who held this view because it seems so outrageous from a practical point of view. But as I did the research for this book, I discovered I was far from alone. Frederick F. Reichheld – author of *The Loyalty Effect* – provides empirical support for the following view of profit.

> Maybe our profit-centered world is as skewed and counterproductive as the concept of an earth-centered universe. That is not to say that profit doesn't matter. Putting the earth in its proper relation to the sun doesn't make the earth less important, or the sun more so. What it did do was make sense of the mechanics. Profit does not have to occupy the center of the business solar system in order to be indispensable.[23]

Interestingly, Reichheld has been inspired by none other than Henry Ford. It should be noted that Henry Ford was successfully sued by a shareholder for lowering the price of Ford cars and raising the wages of employees. Ford believed that higher wages and lower priced automobiles would result in long-run benefit to the company and to American society in general. Note what Ford said about profit: "Business must be run at a profit else it will die. But when anyone tries to run a business solely for profit then also the business must die, for it no longer has a reason for existence."[24]

This philosophy of Henry Ford has not gone unnoticed. In *Built to Last*, an important study by James Collins and Jerry Porras, the authors argue that Ford has done far better than General Motors in terms of profitability and attribute that success to a more appropriate view of profits. Indeed, Collins and Porras entitle chapter 3 "More than Profits."[25]

But Henry Ford is not the only denizen of industry to hold that view. George Merck II, son of the founder of Merck & Company, put it this way:

> I want to. . . express the principles which we in our company have endeavored to live up to. . . . Here is how it sums up. We try to remember that medicine is for the patient. We try never to forget that medicine is for the people. It is not for profits. The profits follow, and if we have remembered that, they have never failed to appear. The better we have remembered it the larger they have been.[26]

Chapter 2 introduced us to Hewlett-Packard as an example of a firm that respected people. Not surprisingly the company understands the paradox of profit. One of the company founders, David Packard, put it this way in a talk to some HP employees:

> I want to discuss *why* a company exists in the first place. In other words why are we here? I think many people assume, wrongly, that a company exists simply to make money. While this is an important result of a company's existence, we have to go deeper and find the real reasons for our being. . . . You can look around [in the general business world] and still see people who are interested in money and nothing else, but the underlying drives come largely from a desire to do something which is of value. So with that in mind, let us discuss why the Hewlett-Packard Company exists. . . . The real reason for our existence is that we provide something which is unique [that makes a contribution].[27]

Packard's view was institutionalized in the company. It is no surprise that the 1998 *Fortune* list of America's most admired companies has Hewlett-Packard in the top ten at number five. Listen to how John Young, HP chief executive from 1976–92, looks at profit.

> Yes, profit is a cornerstone of what we do – it is a measure of our contribution and a means of self-financed growth – but it has never been the *point* in and of itself. The point in fact is to *win* and winning is judged in the eye of the customer and by doing something you can be proud of. There is a symmetry of logic in this. If we provide real satisfaction to real customers – we will be profitable.[28]

Comments like these are not limited to Americans. I discovered a quotation from the Japanese businessman Dr Yoshi Tsurumi who made the same point.

> Most American executives think they are in business to make money, rather than products and service. . . . The Japanese credo, on the other hand, is that a company should become the world's most efficient provider of whatever product and service it offers. Once it becomes the world leader and continues to offer good products, profits follow.[29]

There is still another reason for acting purely out of duty. The view that ethical behavior should be undertaken because it may enhance the bottom line may be called the instrumental use of reason. If the manager claims to act out of duty (because it is right) and is discovered to have acted from self-interest (instrumentally), a high level of cynicism typically results. If managers adopt a strictly instrumental view of ethics, other persons in the firm may as well. The net result may be an overall decrease in ethical behavior. Why? Because if ethics is merely instrumental, what will people do when there is a conflict between doing the right thing and contributing to profit? If ethics is merely instrumental, then there is a real danger that profit rather than ethics will win out. This argument has been forcefully made by Dennis Quinn and Tom Jones.

> If the senior managers of a firm employ ethics "instrumentally" or with "enlightened self-interest" or any other restrictive caveat, why will not employees at lower levels of the firm (or suppliers or customers) also employ ethics instrumentally? Can owners of firms expect ethical restraint from executive managers if the owners show

interest in ethics only because ethics leads to optimum gain for owners? Can you be a "little bit ethical"?[30]

Quinn and Jones express their point by making the choice an exclusive either/or: either it is done for profit, or it is done out of duty. However, even if an action is done for both reasons, I think their basic argument succeeds, since many people think like the most pure Kantians here. For purists, if profit is in the picture, then the appeal to a moral reason is significantly tainted. However, as contemporary Kant scholarship has shown, all Kantian ethics really requires is that the ethical reason be sufficient in the sense that the action would be done even if it did not contribute to profit. Sometimes popular Kantianism is stricter than Kant himself.

This is not merely a theoretical point. There is some evidence that when moral motives are tainted, this has an impact on the behavior of various members of the business organization. For example, there is anecdotal evidence that tainted moral motives have undermined the adoption of teams and the use of quality circles in American corporations. Even if the manager's conscious goal were to increase profits, you can hardly tell the other stakeholders that. Why would an employee want to work harder to increase the wealth of the stockholders? Thus, managers tend to introduce innovations like quality circles on the grounds that the employee is benefited, but if the employee suspects management's motives, the quality circles will not succeed. Interestingly, quality circles have not done well in the USA and one can only wonder if the bottom-line orientation of managers has something to do with it.

We all are familiar with cases where corporate good works are greeted with public scorn because the public is suspicious of the corporation's motives. "They are just trying to buy good will" is a phrase that is often heard. Corporate executives who appear to really act from Kantian motives are frustrated when their motives are questioned. Yet it is hard for the public to tell if an action is performed only in accordance with duty or truly from duty. What evidence can we use to distinguish a company that only appears to act from Kantian motives from one that really does? In these circumstances reputation, corporate character, and a record of altruistic acts are important. If Johnson and Johnson proclaims moral motives for what they do, they are believed. The public remembers how Johnson and Johnson handled the Tylenol poisonings. Not only did they do the right thing but they seemed to think like Kantians. According to a taped interview, James Burke – Johnson and Johnson CEO at the time – said, "We consulted the Credo that put customers first. Thus, there was no question about what to do."

On the other hand, if Exxon proclaims moral motives for what they do they are not believed. The public remembers Exxon's behavior during the Alaskan oil spill. Now if Exxon makes pro-environmental statements they are simply not believed. The public reacted very differently to the Ashland Oil Company after they had a major spill that predated Exxon's. The Ashland management team took responsibility for the spill, admitted past errors (contrary to legal advice not to do so), and paid for the clean-up. In addition, Ashland's CEO flew to the site of the spill near Pittsburgh soon after the spill occurred. There is considerable evidence that management wanted to do the right thing. As a result, Ashland Oil's credibility is higher than Exxon's. However, it seems as if improved credibility was not the motive for Ashland's doing what it did. Of course, we can never be sure and we can be tricked, but we do make these judgments about motivation all the time. That is part of the reason why some companies have better reputations than others. All of this provides evidence for the claim that managers need to take Kant's point about the primacy of moral motives seriously.

A brief summary is in order. I have shown that several companies really do seem to think like Kantians with respect to matters of business ethics. They do the right thing because it is right. In this section I have given arguments to show that such companies are not behaving in a utopian fashion and that other companies might be well served to adopt a Kantian strategy. However, there is much more to be said about the relation of ethics and profit.

Reasons and Emotions: A Brief Aside

Kantian ethics has been criticized as being excessively rationalistic. It does not allow actions arising from moral sentiments (emotions) to count as genuinely moral acts. Even Robert Frank – whose affinity to Kant I cited earlier – builds his theory of ethics on moral sentiments which he specifically contrasts with acting rationally.

(Frank's notion of rationality is limited to instrumental rationality for specific cases.) In fact, Frank subtitles his book "The Strategic Use of the Emotions." Frank thinks the basis of ethics is emotional rather than rational. And one of my examples referred to acting out of love. However, as we know, good acts that are motivated by sympathy or other emotional inclinations are not for Kant genuine moral actions. A visit to a sick friend was only a genuine moral act if the visit was motivated by respect for the categorical imperative.

> To be kind when one can is a duty, and there are, moreover, many persons so sympathetically constituted that without any motive of vanity or selfishness they find an inner satisfaction in spreading joy and rejoice in the contentment of others which they have made possible. But I say that, however dutiful and however amiable it may be, that kind of action has no true moral worth.[31]

One way to handle the problem is to concede that Kant's contention that actions motivated by such emotions or sentiments as kindness or sympathy are not really moral actions is mistaken. Kant really is being excessively rationalistic here. Robert Solomon seems right in his claim that the strict separation of reasons and emotions is an artificial distinction.[32] Perhaps we should count as a moral motive for actions, acting out of the principle of respect for persons and/or acting out of human kindness to another. Indeed, it seems to me that a person who acts out of the principle of respect for persons is likely to be kind and vice versa. Such a reform would certainly make Kantian ethics more acceptable to a host of critics from Bernard Williams to many contemporary feminists. I have no wish to be doctrinaire here. If a company does the right thing because it has the proper ethical climate, I am quite willing to claim that such actions are genuinely moral. However, for the strict Kantian there is still one important argument remaining to show that business people can act from genuine moral motives when issues of ethics are at stake.

Multiple Moral Motives

Suppose we remain pure Kantians with respect to the requirements for motivation of genuinely moral acts. If we do, wouldn't this leave us with at least one unfortunate consequence? Most "corporate good deeds" would not be genuine moral acts because profit is usually a sufficient motivation for the act. Perhaps that is perfectly acceptable. In response to Stuart Hampshire's criticism of Kantian moral motivation, Barbara Herman has argued that Kant does not require us to do every morally worthy act. The categorical imperative functions as a limiting condition by indicating what we cannot do. But so long as the actions of the sympathetic person are in conformity with duty, there is nothing wrong with that. The actions are just not truly moral.[33]

Apply Herman's analysis to the business case. Many actions in business are in conformity with morality but are not done from the motive of morality. There is nothing wrong with that. Thus, we should not think less of a company that sponsors an event like the Walk for Aids in the hopes that they might increase their sales. The company does not deserve any moral credit for their sponsorship but they do not deserve moral condemnation either. Interestingly, many companies have been criticized as doing something wrong for such sponsorship, which shows once again that the genuine public is more of a purist on motivation than Kant himself.

Although this move might have some initial appeal, it is not one I wish to make for three reasons. First, I do not think it would adequately deal with a number of important cases. To begin, consider the recent case of the Marriott Corporation, which first trained and then hired 6,000 welfare recipients, including some homeless people. Why did they do it? Here is what J.W. Marriott, Jr said about the program:

> We're getting good employees for the long term but we're also helping these communities. If we don't step up in these inner cities and provide work, they'll never pull out of it. But it makes bottom line sense. If it didn't, we wouldn't do it.[34]

And a *Business Week* feature article on the Marriott program concludes the same way:

> But this isn't a story about altruism. Marriott's unusual approach to the low-wage dilemma is dictated by corporate self-interest: Helping workers can cut costs and lift productivity. And that goes right to the bottom line.[35]

It certainly appears as if this is a case of an act done in conformity with duty but not out of duty. Yet if you read the full article, the emphasis of the story is on how difficult this effort really is.

> Its [Marriott's] employees drive welfare trainees to work, arrange their day care, negotiate with their landlords, bicker with their case workers, buy them clothes, visit them at home, coach them in everything from banking skills to self-respect – and promise those who stick it out full time jobs at Marriott or elsewhere. Even then, the trainees often show up late, work slowly, fight with co-workers and go AWOL for reasons as simple as a torn stocking.[36]

Kant is rightly famous for his insistence on the burdens of acting out of duty. Certainly, these articles give the sense that for many individuals at Marriott these actions involved tremendous burdens. Despite what J.W. Marriott, Jr says, some people at Marriott are clearly acting out of duty and not merely in conformity with it.

The Marriott Corporation is not alone. Fel-Pro Incorporated of Skokie Illinois has won numerous business ethics awards as a family friendly firm. Fel-Pro is an acknowledged leader in accommodating its business to the complex demands of family life. David Weinberg, Fel-Pro's chairman, describes his company's philosophy as follows:

> Fel-Pro's philosophy toward its employees is incredibly simple. What it says is, for good social reasons and for good business reasons, we ought to treat people honestly, equitably, and openly. And, in return, that comes back to us.[37]

Throughout David Bollier's description of Fel-Pro the emphasis is on the benefits the company has received from the family friendly policy. Yet in reading what they have done, it seems hard to deny that the company's actions are genuinely moral from a Kantian perspective. Management believes that they have an obligation to solve social problems. Here is a list of the actions that the company has done to deserve its place as the premier example of a family friendly firm:

1   It purchased land and then built the Triple R Ranch, a private recreational facility for Fel-Pro employees and their families.

2   Provision of a summer day camp at the Triple R Ranch. Over 300 children attend each summer.

3   On-site day-care center.

4   Five days of subsidized care for ill dependents that allows employees to maintain their work schedules.

5   Assistance in caring for elderly parents through the Illinois Alliance on Aging.

6   Up to $3,300 for any child of an employee accepted at an accredited college or trade school.

7   Up to $3,000 for employees for undergraduate and $6,500 per year for graduate studies. A $1,000 bonus is awarded to a Fel-Pro employee who completes an advanced degree.

8   A tutoring program for the children of employees who are having difficulty in elementary or high school.

9   An on-site fitness and wellness center.

10   A shift that runs from 7:24 a.m. to 3:54 p.m. to minimize the travails of an employee's commute.

11   Up to $5,000 to assist employees with the expenses of adopting a child.

12   Small gifts from the company to commemorate family events such as birthdays, anniversaries, weddings, and births.[38]

There are a dozen reasons why Fel-Pro is regarded as a paradigm example of a family friendly firm. And despite the fact that the management thinks its family friendly philosophy contributes to its success, they also are on record as saying, "This is what society needs and we are part of that society."[39]

After telling the whole story, the fact that Mr Marriott Jr and the Marriott Corporation and the management of Fel-Pro were motivated in part by sound business reasons (profit) seems not to change our desire to ascribe genuine moral worth to their actions. And that leads to the second reason I do not want to accept the suggestion that we simply admit that most corporate good deeds are not genuinely moral because they are not properly motivated. Intuitively, it seems mistaken to say that if the good deed had a plausible business justification and that the good deed would not have been done but for that business reason in addition to the fact that it was the right thing to do, then it is of no moral worth.[40] Even if popular morality would be purist here, a business ethicist ought to pause. Is there any justification for the business ethicist's intuition? Is there any way that Marriott's actions as opposed to the actions of some of its employees could be seen as a genuine moral act in Kant's sense? I think there is one way of perceiving both Marriott's remarks and Fel-Pro's actions that would permit such an interpretation and that way presents a third reason for not accepting the suggestion that most corporate good deeds are not genuinely moral actions.

The moral obligation to make a profit

This third reason is the most important reason of all. The suggestion overlooks the fact that for most managers making a profit is a moral obligation rather than a prudential one. For a publicly held corporation, suppose it is true that the maxim to increase shareholder wealth is a moral obligation. There are many arguments in support of this claim. One that would appeal to a Kantian is that the managers of a publicly held corporation have entered into a contract with the stockholders to do so. Indeed, some have argued that a corporation is nothing but a nexus of contracts.[41] If such a contract does in fact meet the Kantian criteria for a valid contract, e.g., no coercion or deception, a Kantian would insist that it be kept. It should also be noted in passing that nearly all business ethicists accept the claim that increasing shareholder wealth is one of the obligations that business has. Thus, there are very good reasons for business managers like the CEO of Marriott to report that they hired those on welfare because, in part, it was good business. They have a moral obligation to their stockholders and thus they have a moral obligation to provide a business reason for their decisions. Interestingly enough, in a classic article Milton Friedman specifically cites the case of a manager of a publicly held company hiring the hardcore unemployed as an example of unethical action because he is spending someone else's money without their approval.[42] Not only does Wall Street expect a business rationale for corporate good deeds; Wall Street has a moral right to those expectations. This strategy grounds the motive to seek profits in ethics itself.

But this leads to another difficulty. The business person also knows that many people think like purist Kantians. Thus, managers have an incentive to say that they do the act because it is right even when they are doing it for business reasons. Why do Marriott and Fel-Pro say what they do? Do they really believe that part of the reason why they do what they do is because it is right, or do they just say they do it because it is right because that is what the public wants to hear? Suppose it is the latter. The business motive is morally grounded because it is done for profit and managers have an obligation to act profitably, but then paradoxically the announced motive to help is just public relations. And that is what a lot of people think is the case. Motives and intentions are hard to judge, but I think an examination of these cases indicates that part of the reason they do what they do is because they really believe it is right. What Marriott and Fel-Pro are doing seems genuinely moral independently of the fact that it leads to profits.

And so it is. We know from chapter 3 that managers acting on behalf of business have an obligation derived from the imperfect duty to aid others to help solve social problems. This is simply an extension to the corporate level of Kant's claim that an individual has a duty of beneficence. Thus, managers have two duties: to increase shareholder wealth and to aid in the solution of social problems. Now in the Marriott case, the managers can fulfill both duties by hiring people on welfare. They can both contribute to the bottom line and they can aid in solving social problems. If construed this way, Marriott's action is moral even if one is a pure Kantian. (At least so long as Marriott is motivated by its dual obligations.) The cynics are mistaken because they do not recognize the obligation to make a profit as a moral obligation. But if profit-making is a moral obligation, then the clash between morality and profits disappears. There is no clash between the obligations, since both obligations can be fulfilled.

Of course, making the increase in shareholder wealth a moral obligation means that a firm will often face moral conflict. A firm can often aid society only at the expense of profits. What would a Kantian say? First, any solution to the dilemma cannot violate the categorical imperative. That is, a firm can neither choose profits over aid nor aid over profits if such action would be inconsistent or would treat the humanity of persons as a means merely.

So far so good. But one difficulty remains. Those who hold that the manager has a contract with the stockholders to maximize profits might argue as follows: The obligation to keep a contract is a perfect duty. The contract says that profits should not be sacrificed for acts of beneficence. Therefore, a publicly held corporation should only perform beneficent acts when those acts either contribute to profit or are neutral with respect to profit.

The reason we think there is a dilemma here is because we believe that managers are under a contractual and thus a strict obligation to maximize stockholder wealth. Not surprisingly all the suggestions for escaping the dilemma involve a challenge to that belief. First, one can challenge the whole notion that a firm is to be understood as a nexus of contracts and more specifically that the manager has a contract with the shareholders. The former Dean of the Harvard Law School has argued that if any such contract exists, it exists between the manager and the corporate entity itself.[43] On this interpretation, the manager has an obligation to the corporation itself and we unpack that obligation to determine the relation between an obligation to stockholders and an obligation to do good. An interpretation which focused on the corporate entity itself could be consistent with the position that acts of beneficence should either contribute to profit or be neutral with respect to profit. In fact the courts seem to have interpreted the contract in this way.

A second approach would challenge the assumption that the only contractual obligation is to the stockholders.[44] Twenty-nine states now permit managers to consider the interests of other stakeholders in addition to stockholders. A stakeholder theory of the corporation would focus on the various corporate stakeholders and argue that the obligation to the corporate entity is really an obligation to harmonize the interests of the corporate stakeholders. On the stakeholder interpretation, it would be permissible on occasion to sacrifice profits for the interest of another stakeholder. Specifically, it would allow managers to occasionally contribute to solving social problems in communities where the firm operates even if some profits were thereby sacrificed. The chief difficulties with this interpretation include the fact that the federal courts and the courts of the other 31 states have not, by and large, accepted this interpretation and that stakeholder theory has not provided any way of balancing the conflicting stakeholder interests. Stakeholder theory has not been helpful in specific instances of conflict.

Third, others contend that even if a contract does exist between the manager and the stockholders, that contract does not say that managers should always put the maximization of profits ahead of acts of beneficence. Many shareholders approve of management actions which are good for the firm even though profits are not maximized – at least in the short run. And I am aware of no corporation that has polled its stockholders to receive a majority vote on the proposition that the corporation should always sacrifice beneficence to profits whenever the two conflict. It does not seem unreasonable to assume that stockholders in the firms that made *Fortune*'s list of the best 100 firms to work for in America approve of management's policies. Moreover, some mutual funds consist only of companies that are socially responsible and these funds find investors. Thus, there is considerable doubt that most stockholders want managers to maximize short-term profits.[45]

How should a Kantian explicate the relation between the obligation to seek profits and the obligation to contribute to society? It seems to me that the obligation of beneficence at the corporate level is analogous to the obligation of beneficence at the individual level. For both the individual and the corporation, beneficence is an imperfect duty. A corporation is not completely ethical if it does not find occasions to act beneficently. But a corporation need not always act in a beneficent fashion.

However, a corporation's beneficence need not require a sacrifice in profits in order to be genuinely moral. For publicly held corporations I see nothing morally wrong with insisting that beneficence either contribute to profit or at least be neutral with respect to profit. Indeed, for publicly held companies, I think Kantian morality requires that, since there does seem to be a convention approaching a contract or promise that managers have an obligation to increase profits. I also believe that contracts between partners, or among family members, also contain language that would make profits an obligation of those companies. Only the individual proprietorship has no moral obligation to make a profit. For all firms except individual proprietorships, I think Kantian morality is a good corrective to popular morality. Publicly held firms are required to act beneficently on occasion but those beneficent acts must be consistent with the obligation of managers to seek profits.

Thus, we have shown that a corporation – as well as partnerships and family-owned firms – can do good deeds and do those deeds in order to be profitable, and yet those deeds can still have genuine moral worth. For such firms we have explained why corporate executives use the language of ethics and the language of profit-making, and how the use of those two languages does not contaminate the moral worth of what they do. Ironically, it is often the public that is more Kantian than Kant with respect to the purity of motivation.

In the final chapter I turn to Kant's cosmopolitanism and show how the practice of international business can bring about universal moral standards. In this way Kant's optimism regarding gradual moral improvement, at least with respect to business, can be vindicated.

Notes

1 Charles Handy, *Beyond Certainty* (Boston: Harvard Business School Press, 1996), p. 62.
2 Immanuel Kant, *Foundations of the Metaphysics of Morals* 1787 (Indianapolis: Bobbs Merrill, 1969), pp. 9, 15–16.
3 I recall that Tom Donaldson made this criticism at a Tokyo conference in 1990 where I argued that being ethical could provide economic advantages.
4 See N. Dale Wright (ed.) *Papers on the Ethics of Administration* (Provo, Utah: Brigham Young University Press, 1988), pp. 97–120, and *Business Horizons* 34: 4 (July–August 1991), pp. 56–65.
5 Andrew Stark, "What's the Matter with Business Ethics," *Harvard Business Review* May–June, 1993.
6 Immanuel Kant, *Grounding for the Metaphysics of Morals*, in *Ethical Philosophy* (Indianapolis/Cambridge: Hackett Publishing, 1983), p. 10.
7 See the work of Lawrence Kolhberg, for example *The Philosophy of Moral Development* (San Francisco: Harper and Row, 1981).
8 Immanuel Kant, *Lectures on Ethics* (New York: Harper and Row, 1963), p. 16.
9 Immanuel Kant, *The Metaphysics of Morals Part I: The Metaphysical Elements of Justice* 1786 (Indianapolis: Bobbs Merrill, 1965), pp. 20–1.
10 As Thomas E. Hill, Jr has pointed out, even Kant recognized the difficulty in determining the actual motivation for an action. Indeed, Hill argues this difficulty may be one reason why Kant did not emphasize taking account of the moral worth of persons when meting out punishment or in fulfilling one's duty of beneficence. See Hill's

Dignity and Practical Reason in Kant's Moral Theory (Ithaca, NY: Cornell University Press, 1992), pp. 190–5.

11 Immanuel Kant, *Groundwork for the Metaphysics of Morals*, in *Ethical Philosophy* 2nd edn (Indianapolis: Hackett Publishing, 1994), p. 19.

12 Ibid., pp. 13–14.

13 Richard Henson, "What Kant Might Have Said: Moral Worth and the Over-determination of Dutiful Action," *Philosophical Review* 88 (1979), pp. 39–54.

14 Barbara Herman, *The Practice of Moral Judgment* (Cambridge: Harvard University Press, 1993), p. 8.

15 Ibid., p. 12.

16 It should be pointed out that these interpretations of Kant have not won universal acceptance. See, for example, Tom Sorell, "Kant's Good Will and our Nature," *Kant-Studien* 78 (1987), pp. 87–101. In responding to my analysis here, Sorell pointed out, echoing Kant, that we can never be sure that the motive of duty would have been sufficient. Technically, this is correct, although I am perhaps more sanguine than either Kant or Sorell that in many cases we can be highly confident that the motive of duty would have been sufficient.

17 From James O'Toole, *Vanguard Management: Redesigning the Corporate Future* (Garden City, NY: Doubleday, 1985), as quoted in Michael Naughton and Gene R. Laczniak, "A Theological Context of Work," *Journal of Business Ethics* 12 (1993), p. 992.

18 Milton Friedman, "The Social Responsibility of Business Is to Increase Its Profits," *New York Times Magazine* September 13, 1970.

19 Albert Z. Carr, "Is Business Bluffing Ethical?" *Harvard Business Review* (January–February, 1968), pp. 143–53.

20 Robert Frank, *Passions Within Reason* (New York: W.W. Norton, 1988), p. 69.

21 Ibid., p. 253.

22 Immanuel Kant, *Critique of Practical Reason* 1788 (Upper Saddle River, NJ: Prentice-Hall, 1993), pp. 36–7.

23 Frederick F. Reichheld, *The Loyalty Effect* (Boston: Harvard Business School Press, 1996), p. 18.

24 Quoted in ibid., p. 16.

25 James C. Collins and Jerry I. Porras, *Built to Last* (New York: Harper Business, 1994).

26 Quoted in ibid., p. 16.

27 Quoted in ibid., p. 56.

28 Quoted in ibid., p. 57.

29 Quoted in W. Edwards Deming, *Out of the Crisis* (Cambridge, MA: MIT Center for Advanced Engineering Study, 1982), p. 99.

30   Dennis P. Quinn and Thomas M. Jones, "An Agent Morality View of Business Policy," *Academy of Management Review* 20 (1995), p. 28.

31   Immanuel Kant, *Foundations of the Metaphysics of Morals*, pp. 13–14.

32   Robert C. Solomon, *A Passion for Justice* (Reading, MA: Addison-Wesley, 1990).

33   Herman, *The Practice of Moral Judgment*, chapter 2

34   Dana Milbank, "Hiring Welfare People, Hotel Chain Finds, Is Tough But Rewarding," *Wall Street Journal* October 31, 1996, p. A1.

35   Catherine Young, "Low-Wage Lessons," *Business Week* November 11, 1996, p. 116.

36   Ibid. The *Business Week* article describes in detail the extent to which Marriott's managers and supervisors have had to function as baby sitters.

37   Quoted in David Bollier, *Aiming Higher* (New York: American Management Association, 1996), p. 224.

38   As reported in ibid., pp. 226–31.

39   Quoted in ibid., p. 230.

40   This argument was provided to me by Tom Sorell.

41   Michael Jensen and W.H. Meckling, "Theory of the Firm: Managerial Behavior, Agency Costs, and Ownership Structure," *Journal of Financial Economics* 3 (October, 1976), pp. 305–60.

42   Milton Friedman, "The Social Responsibility of Business Is to Increase Its Profits."

43   Robert C. Clark, "Agency Costs versus Fiduciary Duties," in John W. Pratt and Richard J. Zeckhauser (eds) *Principles, Agents: The Structure of Business* (Boston: Harvard Business School Press, 1985), pp. 55–79.

44   The view that managers have contractual obligations to other stakeholders is defended by William M. Evan and R. Edward Freeman in "A Stakeholder Theory of the Modern Corporation: Kantian Capitalism," in Tom L. Beauchamp and Norman E. Bowie (eds) *Ethical Theory and Business* (Englewood Cliffs, NJ: Prentice Hall, 1993), pp. 75–84.

45   I admit that many institutional investors are legally required to be more short-term oriented and that these institutional investors are a potent force in the market.

5

The Cosmopolitan Perspective

Since the narrower or wider community of the peoples of the earth
has developed so far that a violation of rights in one place is felt
throughout the world, the idea of a law of world citizenship is no
high flown or exaggerated notion. It is a supplement to the unwrit-
ten code of the civil and international law, indispensable for the
maintenance of the public human rights and hence also of perpetual
peace. (Immanuel Kant)

Introduction

One of the key features of the Enlightenment was its cosmopolitan
perspective. Enlightenment thinkers were strongly critical of religious and nationalistic values, since they believed that local customs
and religious doctrines interfered with the development of a cosmopolitan spirit. One of the great strengths of the Enlightenment was
its claim that all human beings were endowed with reason. Another
strength was its ability to see beyond national boundaries. Charles
Beitz has characterized Kant as a cosmopolitan in the sense that
national boundaries have at most a derivative significance for him.
What is of most concern to Kant is the universal human community. The internal activities of a state are subject to moral criticism
from those outside it and the citizens of any given state may have
obligations that extend beyond national boundaries. Kant is cosmopolitan in that sense.[1] As Terry Nardin has said:

It was one of the great achievements of eighteenth-century European
thought on international relations that it was able to articulate the

idea that international society is defined by the deference of states, despite various differences, to the authority of a common body of practices and rules. . . . Thinkers from Montesquieu and Voltaire to Burke, Martens, and Kant were able with increasing clarity to recognize the society of states as a distinct historical institution, one not to be confused with the great society of mankind.[2]

Capitalism is also cosmopolitan in its outlook and thus supports Enlightenment cosmopolitanism. Capitalism pulls in the opposite direction from nationalism and religious sectarianism. In fact many writers argue that it is economic relations among people from different countries that provides the basis for an international ethic. As we shall see, Kant appears to be in this tradition. As R.J. Vincent has argued:

This cosmopolitanist morality is not put forward merely as an appeal to our better natures or to our capacity to understand history as the working out of some moral scheme for humankind. It is an appeal also to a set of facts that has at least as much claim to our attention as that which underpins the morality of states. Against the division of the world into separate political communities, it places their amalgamation in a common economic community. There is a complex network of economic interactions in contemporary world society whose existence the writers on transnationalism and interdependence (and dependence) have tried to come to terms with. The existence of this network invalidates any claim on behalf of the society of states that it marks the boundaries of social cooperation.[3]

Economic cooperation also provides the foundation of a universal morality. Charles Beitz has cited Kant as one who believes that "international economic cooperation creates a new basis for international morality."[4]

In this chapter I shall indicate how Kant's cosmopolitanism is related to international business. In so doing I shall return to some of the themes in chapters 1 and 2. Especially important in this discussion will be Kant's concept of universality. First, I shall show that there is a universal market morality which cuts across the boundaries of all countries. As international trade expands, this market morality will become a common feature of international trade worldwide. The argument for the existence of this market morality will be based on the first formulation of the categorical imperative. In the last part of the chapter I shall demonstrate how international capitalism can be supportive of Kant's ideal of perpetual peace as well as of democracy and human rights.

The Morality of the Market

A central issue in international business ethics is the problem of relativism. In everyday language, the issue is: when in Rome should you do as the Romans do? The Kantian theory of capitalism has a ready answer to this question and it is not quite so foundationalist as you would think. As I argued in chapter 1, a practice not in violation of the categorical imperative is morally permissible. So long as an action would not be self-defeating if universalized, does not treat the humanity in persons merely as means but as an end in itself, and can be publicly advocated so that it was acceptable to all members of the moral community, it is morally permissible. Obviously, different cultures could adopt some different moral principles and yet the principles of both would pass the tests of the categorical imperative.

However, there are some practices that should not be acceptable within a capitalist framework because these practices could not pass the test of the categorical imperative. Arguments for this point and the identification of such practices are found in my discussion of the first formulation of the categorical imperative in chapter 1. The notion that there are some universal norms for capitalist business practice is not limited to me. As is well known, Tom Donaldson defends a list of fundamental rights.[5] Richard DeGeorge says this about international business ethics:

> There are also basic norms necessary for the conduct of business such as keeping promises, honoring contracts, telling the truth, and respecting the lives and integrity of those with whom one engages in business. Even on issues of extortion and gross bribery there is a general consensus that these are wrong, even though prevalent and tolerated in some countries.[6]

I believe DeGeorge is correct and Kantian moral philosophy provides the theoretical rationale for those assertions.

What is significant is that as capitalism becomes accepted throughout the world, the morality that makes capitalism possible will be accepted as well. As an empirical matter we should begin to see an increasing number of attempts to achieve international standards of business ethics. Our arguments here will run parallel to those in chapter 1. First I shall show that certain business practices are in violation of the universalizability requirement of the categorical imperative. I shall then hypothesize that as markets become truly international, these practices that violate the categorical imperative will die out. I will then cite evidence to show that international agreements are being instituted to outlaw these practices and that as a matter of fact their incidence is declining.

Bribery

Let us begin with business practices that violate the categorical imperative. Certainly one of the most discussed ethical issues in international business ethics is the issue of bribery. (For purposes of this discussion bribery is distinguished from extortion and facilitating payments.) If a maxim permitting bribery were universalized, it could not pass the test of the categorical imperative. And in some instances, bribery would be economically inefficient as well. Consider cases where bribery both increases transaction costs and distorts efficiency. Imagine a company offering a bribe. Suppose the company could have received the contract on the merits of its product without paying the bribe. If so, paying bribes adds to its costs and it will lose out to competitors that have equally good products but incur less costs since they do not bribe. Other things being equal, companies that do not bribe have a competitive advantage that will drive companies offering a bribe out of business. Since every company has as its fundamental purpose staying in business, a company that offers a bribe is engaged in a pragmatic contradiction. Publicly held companies have a moral obligation to stay in business and make a profit, thus the offering of bribes by a publicly held company rests on a maxim that results in a pragmatic contradiction and is wrong.

Now consider the case of a company that accepts a bribe. In so doing it is receiving a product of less quality than it would have received for the same expenditure. That puts the company that receives a bribe at a competitive disadvantage such that, other things being equal, companies receiving a bribe will be driven out of business. But since every company has as its fundamental purpose staying in business, receiving a bribe places the company in a pragmatic contradiction. Since publicly held companies have a moral obligation to stay in business and make a profit, a company that receives a bribe acts on a maxim that results in a pragmatic contradiction and is wrong.

Unfortunately, as Ed Soule has pointed out to me, many bribes are not inefficient in this sense. This is especially true when bribery is a small portion of a firm's cost structure and thus has a relatively small effect on total firm cost and competitiveness. As Soule points out, suppose two aircraft manufacturers produce a plane for a $100 million. Firm A provides $5 million for marketing, while firm B provides $5 million for bribes. In cases like this there is no impact of bribery on efficiency. Indeed, for some products (e.g., commercial and military aircraft) it may actually be more efficient to bribe than to market. That is what makes bribery in these cases so difficult to eliminate.

But bribery in these cases is also morally wrong and in violation of the categorical imperative. The problem with bribery is that it distorts value between parties. That is, the buyer is denied a portion of value that is siphoned off by the bribe-taker. In this case bribery is tantamount to theft. Likewise with the receiving of bribes. Normally the recipient is not the company but an individual acting in her own capacity. In these cases economically a bribe functions like a discount. However, it also still functions as a kind of theft. Thus, the arguments from chapter 1 showing that theft is in violation of the first formulation of the categorical imperative apply here. As you recall, that argument showed that if there were a sufficient amount of theft, the system of private property would be undermined. Thus, you would expect responsible business people to band together and urge that bribery be treated as an unacceptable business practice. As I argue later in this chapter, this is exactly what is happening in the international arena.

The above arguments assume that bribery is not a common practice in the country under discussion. If bribery were the norm the argument breaks down. Even in cases where transaction cost arguments apply, there is no conceptual contradiction involved when everyone bribes. If everyone accepts and pays bribes in a given country, no single company can get a niche as a nonbribe giver or nonbribe taker since no one will do business with it.

However, that situation moves the argument to a higher level. A nation or culture where bribery is the norm will be at a competitive disadvantage with respect to a nation or culture where a norm against bribery prevails. The widespread existence of bribery interferes with the development of an adequate standard of living. Widespread bribery in many African countries is often cited as one of the reasons for those countries' low level of economic development. There is clear economic evidence that bribery inflicts high social costs on a society and the more extensive the bribery the higher these costs are. Steve Hanke, a Johns Hopkins University economist, has found the following results in a study for the Joint Economic Committee of Congress: a combination of factors including the absence of currency controls, strong property rights, and a lack of official corruption and bribery constitute the economic freedom index. For every 10 percent increase in the economic freedom index, Hanke found a corresponding 7.4–13.6 percent rise in per capita income.[7] Admittedly the effect of bribery is not disaggregated from the above measure. But consider this: the Luigi Einaudi research center has estimated that corruption has inflated Italy's government debt by $200 billion. After the systematic attack on corruption in the early 1990s, bids for public works projects were coming in about 40 percent below cost estimates, which results in a saving of $4.4 billion in 1993.[8]

Given that bribery interferes with the duty of a government's officials to enhance the economic well-being of its citizens, it is morally wrong. Since it does interfere with the well-being of the average citizen there will be demands that it be stopped. Since bribery is also inefficient as an economic practice or is tantamount to theft, which in theory threatens the regime of private property, we can assume that multinationals will seek agreements outlawing bribery and that as competitive markets spread throughout the world bribery will decrease. Significantly, all the cross-cultural business codes discussed below have provisions outlawing bribery. For example, the 1977 International Chamber of Commerce code was adopted to combat bribery and extortion. And the OECD 1976 guidelines for multinationals contained a provision urging multinationals to refrain from bribery regardless of where they were doing business. This OECD provision was strengthened in May of 1994 with the adoption of the "Recommendation on Bribery in International Business Transactions." Under that recommendation there will be annual peer reviews of all OECD countries.[9] Given the immorality and inefficiency of bribery, we can predict that it will decrease under international capitalism.

Discrimination

One highly immoral practice that is found in various societies around the world is discrimination, be it based on religion, sex, ethnicity, or the color of one's skin. Many argue that discrimination, particularly against women, is rampant in certain companies and in certain countries. Such discrimination is in clear violation of the respect for persons formulation of the categorical imperative. Moreover, one kind of discrimination in the market violates the first formulation of the categorical imperative as well. It involves a pragmatic contradiction. This argument proceeds in a way parallel to the argument against some forms of bribery.

The first step in the argument is to show that discrimination by a given company puts that company at a competitive disadvantage. That point was made over 35 years ago by Milton Friedman:

> There is an economic incentive in a free market to separate economic efficiency from other characteristics of the individual. A businessman or entrepreneur who expresses preferences in his business activity that are not related to productive efficiency is at a disadvantage compared to other individuals who do not. Such an individual is imposing higher costs on himself than are other individuals who do not have such preferences. Hence in a free market they will tend to drive him out. The man who objects to buying from or working alongside a Negro, for example, thereby limits his range of choice. He will generally have to pay a higher price for what he buys or receive a lower return for his work. Or, put the other way, those of us who regard color of skin or religion as irrelevant can buy some things more cheaply as a result.[10]

Given that discrimination puts one at a competitive disadvantage, a firm that discriminates on bases other than productivity, price, or quality, puts itself at a competitive disadvantage. Other things being equal, in the long run it will be put out of business. Since surviving in business and making a profit is the essential purpose of business, a maxim of discrimination is self-defeating. For publicly held companies surviving in business and making a profit is a moral obligation, so a manager in a publicly held corporation who discriminates does so on a pragmatically contradictory maxim that makes his action morally wrong.

Of course, discrimination is usually a societal problem rather than just an institutional one. But a society that discriminates puts itself at a disadvantage as well. In the old Soviet Union women physicians were a commonplace. In the United States, however, women were encouraged to be nurses rather than physicians – at least until fairly recently. Not using the capabilities of 50 percent of the population is a serious drain on efficiency. Indeed, corporations have become some of the most ardent defenders of contemporary affirmative action programs. There are pragmatic reasons for having a work force that resembles the business population. I recall at an Academy of Management meeting hearing former Atlanta Mayor Andrew Young describe how Atlanta captured the 1996 Olympics from Miami. Young knew the ethnic composition of the selection committee and was sure to have each person spend time with an Atlantan he or she could identify with. As Young said, "Until then I hadn't realized we had Poles in Atlanta." Young contrasted the Atlanta approach with the all-white business group that represented Miami. Who said a Kantian could not accommodate difference?

If these types of arguments have merit, we should expect to see greater tolerance and less discrimination throughout the world, and we should find the least amount of discrimination in capitalist countries and in times of greatest economic prosperity. And so we do.

Honesty and trust

Yet another example concerns honesty in business relationships. We have already seen from chapter 1 that economic exchange requires the keeping of contracts. In the international context some might argue that the centrality of contracts in business relationships is a thoroughly Western idea. Many Eastern countries proceed on the basis of a handshake rather than a formal contract. Thus, contract-making is not essential to capitalist business enterprises.

The thrust of this argument is correct. However, where handshakes replace the contract, trust is the glue that holds the relationship together. We have already shown in chapter 1 that actions that have the effect of undermining trust result in pragmatic contradictions and thus fail the test of the first formulation of the categorical imperative.

As a last example to strengthen the conclusion reached in chapter 1 and to show the application of trust in a cosmopolitan context, let us consider the growth of trust in people who are not like us. The empirical evidence shows that we tend be more trusting of those people who are like us and less trusting of those who are not like us. As international business expands this attitude will have to change. International firms do business in many diverse cultures and increasingly they will be entering partnerships or strategic alliances with people very different from themselves. One way for this type of trust to develop is to focus on the similarity that exists among professions or business functions. For example, as Ed Soule has pointed out, a foreign currency trader in Hong Kong has more in common with a foreign currency trader in London than he has with his next door neighbor, and a divisional controller for IBM in Austin has more in common with an IBM divisional controller in Germany than she does with her aunt in Des Moines. Thus, international capitalism does have this homogenizing and leveling effect that makes the development of trust among people from different ethnic backgrounds possible. This anecdotal evidence is buttressed by academic research. Scholars have been concerned with how trust is possible among people in temporary business relationships, e.g., audit teams, juries, civic commissions, and actors. Dawes has argued that this trust is possible because we have confidence in the role that John plays rather than in John. Thus, if I am a quality control engineer, and I meet John who is a quality control engineer but from a different ethnic background, then I can trust John because he is a quality control engineer. The fact that he is from a different ethnic background does not matter.[11] Thus, companies that are both trusting and trustworthy can gain a competitive advantage here.

Of course, a company should try to discriminate between those potential partners who are trustworthy and those who aren't. To trust those who are not worthy of trust is a foolish and ultimately fatal business strategy. However, failure to trust merely because a potential partner is of a different race, religion, or ethnic origin is also a foolish and ultimately fatal business strategy. A quotation from an Indian-born engineer captures both the spirit of contemporary international business and the cosmopolitan Enlightenment ideal: "My body was made in India, my science learned in England. A heterogeneous trusting culture like the United States should give us an advantage over homogeneous non-trusting cultures.[12]

If international strategic alliances are essential for business success, then a multinational should pursue the means for success and for publicly held multinationals this pursuit is a moral obligation, not just a prudential one. If an appropriate trusting attitude and trustworthy actions are required for this success they are moral requirements as well. Failure to do so involves the managers of the firm in a pragmatic contradiction.

Empirical evidence for universal norms

If this analysis is correct, we should see evidence for an increasing number of international business codes of conduct that seek to prohibit practices like bribery and discrimination, and which seek to build trust among international trading partners.

William Frederick has done an exhaustive study of transnational corporate codes.[13] He found considerable overlap. Another study conducted by Catherine Langlois and Bodo Schlegelmilch focused on company codes of conduct in Europe. Although the authors did find many differences among the codes, they nonetheless concluded:

> Many ethical issues transcend national barriers. Fairness and honesty in a company's relations to the public are found in the corporate codes of ethics on both sides of the Atlantic. . . . Thus companies in Europe and the US ban the acceptance of gifts or bribes, promote the use of accurate records, and warn against conflict of interest.[14]

Recently a group of Minnesota businesspersons under the auspices of the Minnesota Center on Corporate Responsibility developed a set of principles for the practice of international business. These principles were taken to the Caux Roundtable, an international organization of American, European, and Japanese businesspersons. The Japanese moral concept of *keosei* was added and these principles were then renamed the Caux Principles for the Conduct of International Business. These principles speak specifically to issues of trust and discrimination and the notion of *keosei* is designed to build trust. Now endorsement of the Caux principles is being sought from an even wider audience. The principles recently have been translated into Chinese and Arabic.

There is also a growing attempt to establish international norms when specific international business ethics issues arise. You may recall that various clothing manufacturers and makers of athletic footwear were strongly criticized for having plants or suppliers who had plants that paid sweatshop wages. Criticism was also leveled at retailers who sold their products. In an attempt to deal with this issue, the Council on Economic Priorities and a group of major business firms have come up with a common set of standards called Social Accountability 8000 or SA 8000. They require that plants meet the following standards:

1   No child or forced labor.
2   A safe working environment.
3   Recognition of the right of workers to form a union.
4   Usually work no more than a 48-hour week.
5   Pay a wage sufficient to meet basic needs.

The agreement which went into effect October 7, 1997 included both US and foreign companies, including Avon, Eileen Fisher, Sainsbury, Toys R Us and Otto Versand, as well as the accounting firms KPMG-Peat Marwick and SGS-ICS.[15] These standards are meant to resemble the quality auditing standards of the International Standards Organization which are in use in 80 countries. Adoption of the plan requires that signatory firms' plants be certified. KPMG-Peat Marwick has already published a brochure advertising their services as a certifier. *Business Week*, where this information appeared, described the results as follows: "The CEP effort represents a potential breakthrough not just on sweatshops but on common labor standards for the global economy as a whole."[16]

The existence of a marketplace morality is significant because it shows that international business can be governed by a set of rules and procedures that will hold constant across different cultures. Some rules and procedures of a marketplace morality must be followed by a certain threshold of businesses if capitalism is to exist. Other rules and procedures will evolve as various countries negotiate the rules for good international business practice. Thus, in every capitalist country there should be a common set of rules and practices which govern economic exchange. What this implies is that if Romans are to do business with the Japanese, then whether in Rome or Tokyo, there is a morality to which members of the business community must subscribe – even if the Japanese and Romans differ on other issues of morality.

If this analysis is correct, an issue of some controversy in international business ethics will become less important. The so-called "When you are in Rome, do you do as the Romans do?" problem will take care of itself. If there is, as I have argued, a capitalist market morality, and if following the norms of a market morality provides firms with a competitive advantage over both, the differences between business morality in Tokyo, New York, and Rome will begin to disappear. Violations of the first formulation of the categorical imperative are, when universalized, self-defeating in international business as well.

International Business Can Contribute to World Peace, Universal Rights, and Democracy

The effect of capitalism on the quality of life has been much debated. Albert O. Hirschman has classified the views as civilizing, destructive, or feeble.[17] The thinkers of the Enlightenment, including Kant, have generally tended toward the civilizing camp. More specifically Kant, along with several of his contemporaries, believed that commerce contributed to world peace, to universal moral values, and to the establishment of democracy. Let us see how Kant defended these claims.

Commerce supports world peace

It was a main contention of the Enlightenment that a cosmopolitan worldview supported by international commerce would also support world peace. For the Enlightenment, war was the greatest evil — an evil caused in part by an excessively fervent nationalism. Early capitalist supporters of free trade, which included a large number of philosophers, believed that international commerce provided a means for linking together the nations of the world peacefully and democratically. As John Stuart Mill (1848) said:

> It is hardly possible to overate the value, in the present low state of human improvement, of placing human beings in contact with persons dissimilar to themselves and with modes of thought and action unlike those with which they are familiar. Such communication has always been and is peculiarly in the present age, one of the primary sources of progress.[18]

And as the nations of the world conduct business with one another they will behave like one another. As David Hume put it:

> Where several neighboring nations have a very close communication together, either by policy, commerce, or traveling, they acquire a similitude of manners, proportioned to the communication.[19]

Both the founder of capitalism Adam Smith and Kant saw the connection between commerce and world peace. Smith said:

> At the particular time when these discoveries were made, the superiority of force happened to be so great on the side of the Europeans, that they were enabled to commit with impunity every sort of injustice in those remote countries. Hereafter, perhaps, the natives of those countries may grow stronger, or those of Europe may grow weaker, and the inhabitants of all the different quarters of the world may arrive at the equality of courage and force which, by inspiring mutual fear, can alone overawe the injustice of independent nations into some sort of respect for the rights of one another. But nothing seems more likely to establish this equality of force than that mutual communication of knowledge and all sorts of improvements which an extensive commerce from all countries to all countries naturally, or rather necessarily, carries along with it.[20]

Kant expressed the same sentiments:

> In the end, war itself will be seen as not only so artificial, in outcome so uncertain for both sides, in aftereffects so painful in the form of an

ever-growing war debt (a new invention) that cannot be met, that it will be regarded as a most dubious undertaking. The impact of any revolution on all states on our continent, so clearly knit together through commerce will be so obvious that other states, driven by their own danger but without any legal basis, will offer themselves as arbiters, and thus they will prepare the way for a distant international government for which there is not precedent in world history.[21]

In these quotations we have the standard views of the Enlightenment. We should emphasize the ways in which people are alike rather than the ways in which they are different. Emphasizing difference produces conflict. Commerce is a way of bringing people together rather than keeping them apart. If commerce is successful in bringing people together, then the chances for peace among nations improve.

Kant believed that international commerce supported world peace and interestingly that view is very much alive today. During the 1970s and 1980s Americans defended US trade agreements with the Soviet Union on the grounds they would decrease the likelihood of war. Today, the same arguments are used to encourage trade with Russia and the other former Soviet republics and for the granting of most favored nation treatment to China. In another world trouble spot, some are arguing that peace between Jordan, PLO-ruled areas, and Israel will be maintained and nurtured by increasing trade and business dealings. A 1991 *Fortune* article proposed a Mideast Common Market as a cure for fighting in the Mideast. In that article, Israeli Staff Wertheimer, who owns Ivcar Corporation, a $300 million a year producer of machine tools, says he has employed Arab workers for 30 years. "In our plants and offices, Arabs and Jews work side by side to make products instead of mischief." Even after the assassination of Yithak Rabin, the same argument was being made.

During the Rabin years, Israeli business executives, for the first time, prospected openly in such Arab states as Tunisia, Saudi Arabia, Oman, Qatar and Bahrain – none of which have diplomatic relations with Israel. Many of their Arab hosts then visited Israel. In Jordan some 80,000 tourists have come through, without incident, since Jordan and Israel made piece a year ago. About 35,000 Jordanians have visited Israel. Israeli companies work in Jordan in mining, textile manufacturing, and real estate development. . . . Peace and business can turn things upside down. David Kimche, a longtime agent of Mossad, the Israeli intelligence service, and a former general of the foreign ministry, spent years looking at Arabs as enemies, he says, and at Yasser Arafat "as the epitome of everything evil." Now, Mr Kimche, who has traveled to several Gulf Arab states as chairman of a firm that tries to interest companies in Israeli technology, sees Arab nations as markets and the Palestinian leader as an "ally to reach peace," he says.[22]

Now I must admit that the evidence here is not universal. There are certainly instances where trading partners do go to war with one another. Germany has gone to war twice in this century with its European trading partners. However, after the conflict in Vietnam, the major trading partners have been very reluctant to enter into war. My children were the first to grow up without having to face the prospect of being drafted to fight in a foreign war. The actions against Iraq, although led by the USA, resulted from an international coalition. So although these examples provide a basis for hope more than irrefutable evidence, at long last Kant may be right: war among the industrialized countries has become too destructive, too expensive, and too economically irrational.

Capitalism supports democratic institutions

Finally, capitalism can be supportive of democratic institutions so that liberal societies are often described today as capitalist democracies. As Fukuyama has argued:

> But in the long run the industrialization process itself necessitates a more highly educated population and a more complex division of labor, both of which tend to be supportive of democratic political institutions.[23]

It should also be noted that there are few moderately wealthy capitalist countries that are not democracies. However, there certainly have been times in history when countries have been both wealthy capitalist countries and authoritarian, as is seen in Germany in the 1930s and 1940s. Some countries in Southeast Asia today – such as Burma – are capitalist and yet authoritarian. However, thinkers like Milton Friedman, Friedrich Von Hayek, and Francis Fukuyama argue that there are no democracies with centrally planned economies. If this empirical generalization were to hold, capitalism would be a necessary condition for a democracy, but not a sufficient one.

One of the strongest proponents of the view that capitalism is supportive of democratic institutions is Milton Friedman. In *Capitalism and Freedom* he writes:

> Economic arrangements play a dual role in the promotion of a free society. On the one hand, freedom in economic arrangements . . . is an end in itself. In the second place, economic freedom is also an indispensable means toward the achievement of political freedom.[24]

For example, Friedman points out that freedom of speech is more meaningful as long as alternative opportunities for employment exist. However, these alternatives are impossible if the government owns and operates the means of production. In a private diversified economic community someone has a better chance to publish views that are contrary to the views of a given editor, government, or even majority of the public. If one can find some audience that is interested, then one can usually find a publisher, even one who disagrees with the views of the author. After all, what the publisher really wants to do is to make a profit. Opportunities for profit often overcome the distaste for certain ideas.

Friedman argues that capitalist economic institutions are supportive of democratic institutions in another way as well. In capitalist economic institutions economic transactions are individual and voluntary. In principle, no one enters an exchange unwillingly. Political decisions, on the other hand, and even in democracies, are coercively enforced on the minority. Persons who do not believe that the expenditures by government for national defense or education are correct must nevertheless submit to the majority. Whenever a decision that could be made in the market is made in the political arena, an unnecessary element of coercion is added.[25] As coercion is increased, the losers (minority) become more resentful. This increases social tension and creates strains in the social fabric that can threaten democratic institutions.

Another argument has been advanced by Francis Fukuyama in his book *The End of History and the Last Man* and reiterated in *Trust*. Fukuyama believes that human beings are not only motivated by material gain but are also motivated by a desire for recognition. He expresses this desire for recognition in almost Kantian terms:

> All human beings believe they have a certain inherent worth or dignity. When that worth is not recognized adequately by others, they feel anger; when they do not live up to others' evaluation, they feel shame; and when they are evaluated appropriately, they feel pride.[26]

Fukuyama then uses this universal desire for recognition as a main premise in his argument for the relation between capitalism and democracy. Fukuyama argues that before capitalism the struggle for recognition manifested itself in the struggle for political dominance, often under the guise of nationalism or religion. What capitalism provides is another arena for the struggle for recognition to take place. This in turn allows the possibility for less bloody struggle in the political arena and for democratic institutions to arise.

> Modern liberal democracy seeks to satisfy this desire for recognition by basing the political order on the principle of universal and equal recognition. But in practice liberal democracy works because the struggle for recognition that formerly had been carried out on a military, religious, or nationalist plane is now pursued on an economic one. Where formerly princes sought to vanquish each other by risking their lives in bloody battles, they now risk their capital through the building of industrial empires. . . . In Japan this happened directly as the samurai or warrior class was capitalized in what amounted to a buyout of their social status, and turned to business.[27]

This Enlightenment vision of the earth as a family bound together in peace by economic bonds clashes with the views of those who blame capitalist institutions for war. This argument should also be heard by those ethical theories (the advocates of particularity) that insist on the importance of emphasizing what distinguishes groups. Some argue that liberal democracy and capitalism are the only viable means of organizing political and economic institutions in the modern world. Democracy is the accepted international standard as the legitimate state. The collapse of the Soviet Union has eliminated the only competitor of capitalism as a means of organizing economic life. (Capitalism itself, of course, comes in many varieties, with American, German, and Japanese models as most dominant.)

Objections and Replies

Despite these arguments, many contemporary intellectuals see capitalism as destructive rather than civilizing. Many contemporary American intellectuals have criticized the cosmopolitan "we are all one human family" perspective of Kant. Rather than celebrate our common humanity, our differences should be the cause of celebration. To do justice to these criticisms would require a separate book of its own. However, as this study comes to a close a few points regarding these criticisms should be kept in mind.

Let us begin by considering the criticisms made against the Enlightenment emphasis on humankind in general. Particularist opponents of Kant argue that we should celebrate ethnicity and other forms of diversity and they criticize Enlightenment thinkers, especially Kant, who ignore it. And these critics argue capitalism makes things worse rather than better because capitalism imposes a uniformity of wants around the world. These critics would quote with disapproval the remark of H.J. Heinz's CEO Anthony Reilly: "Once television is there, people of whatever shade, culture, or origin want roughly the same things."[28] Sometimes this criticism is captured by the term "the McDonaldization of the Planet" or simply "McWorld." Many critics of international capitalism decry the uniformity that is found everywhere. To this aesthetic critique, the critics often raise an issue of justice as well. They argue that the spread of modernization exemplified by international capitalism threatens to destroy the culture of indigenous people around the globe. The critics object to the imposition of a market economy on traditional cultures in the name of development. What can be said in response?

I begin by pointing out that this universalist outlook is hardly the exclusive province of white Western males.[29] One quotation, from Kwame Anthony Appiah speaks for many:

We will only solve our problems if we see them as human problems arising out of a special situation, and we shall not solve them if we see them as African problems, generated by our being somehow unlike others.[30]

The first point to be made is that not all diversity is good. It may be good that certain tribes in the Amazon survive. It would not be good that a tribe of Nazis survive, or at least it is not self-evidently good. What types of diversity are moral goods requires a moral theory to distinguish good diversity from bad. And it is just this overarching set of criteria which universalist theories like Kant's are designed to provide.

Moreover, even within indigenous culture, there are characteristics which most critics of international capitalism would want to change. For example, few would deny the benefits of the Merck drug Mectizan described in chapter 4 to the members of those indigenous tribes that suffer from river blindness. The life spans in these tribes are far below the average of more developed countries. Should the benefits of modern medicine be denied those people in the name of maintaining the purity of the culture?[31]

The debate between the relativists and the universalists on this question has grown especially intense. Amartya Sen and Martha Nussbaum have developed a theory of central human capabilities meant to apply across cultures.[32] Cultures and institutions that contribute to the development and flourishing of those capabilities are good; cultures and institutions that do not are bad. Now, Onora O'Neill has shown how Kantian ethics is compatible with the Sen/Nussbaum approach. One can further test the list of human capabilities against the categorical imperative. If one could not will the development of the capability in everyone, that capability cannot be defended on moral grounds. On the other hand, capabilities that one can will everyone develop are morally permissible. O'Neill puts it this way:

> When we then ask which capabilities could in principle be secured for all, we discover that some capabilities cannot be achieved for all. These are capabilities that need and create victims; they are unjust capabilities. Other capabilities can be enjoyed by all, and when they are, will reduce vulnerability. . . . The capabilities which can justly be secured are capabilities that will reduce and tend to eliminate the possibility of violence, coercion, deception, depression and the like, since these latter capabilities embody principles that *could not* be followed by all. For example, the injustice of a "head of family's"

capability to prevent his dependents from undertaking activity outside the home, is evident from the fact that this capability cannot be
extended to all.[33]

Thus, persons following a capabilities approach or a Kantian
approach have criteria for judging cultural practices. Cultural practices which fail to pass those moral tests should disappear, just as the
immoral practices in our own culture should disappear. Those who
find this to be an exercise in Western moral imperialism will need
argument both against these universalist positions and against those
who point out that the relativist position seems to condone all kinds
of injustices.

Let us directly confront the challenge to economic international-
ism. As a practical matter modernization will come to indigenous
people and only hopeless romantics would think otherwise. Even
persons who are not especially sympathetic to capitalism recognize
that modernity is challenging all traditional cultures. For example,
Seyla Benhabib writes:

> Since the fifteenth and sixteenth centuries, what was once the unique
> and peculiar experience of the West's confrontation with modernity,
> has today become globalized. The encounter between tradition
> and modernity, the imperative of nation states to survive in a world
> economic system, to maintain growth, to participate in international
> means of communication, production, commerce, and transport, not
> to mention armaments, have all created the inevitability of moder-
> nity. . . . The situation today is that of a world-wide confrontation
> and interchange between the imperatives of tradition and modernity.
> This confrontation undermines the posture of bemused detachment
> which the cultural relativist would like to assume. . . . In the process
> of world-wide communication and modernization, there are only
> participants who exert moral claims upon each other.[34]

Moreover, many of these critics of modernity seem guilty of a
kind of paternalistic arrogance. McDonalds is successful because
huge numbers of people want the product McDonalds offers. Of
course, the fact that people want the product does not settle the
issue as to whether it is really good to have it. However, the current
way of settling issues like this is through democratic procedures.
That is how we have decided to make heroin illegal. Now if a vote

were taken in Japan on the question of whether or not to allow fast food chains, the vast majority of Japanese would vote in favor of the chains. And so would the vast majority of most people in most countries of the world. A minority may not like "McWorld" and they have every right to try to convince the majority that they are mistaken, but they certainly do not have the right to impose their views on others.

Enlightenment thinkers have always been concerned with the tendency of ethnicity to lead to war. It is one thing to celebrate one's heritage, religious or ethnic. It is quite another to hate those who have a religious or ethnic heritage that is different. In areas of the world where you find a lack of economic opportunity and ethnic divisions, you tend to have ethnic strife. As Fukuyama has noted, capitalist institutions provide another opportunity for socialization. A person can identify with his or her company as well as with his or her ethnic brethren. As he says:

> In developing capitalist countries with strong civil societies . . . the economy itself is the locus of a substantial part of social life. When one works for Motorola, Siemens, Toyota, or even a small family dry cleaning business, one is part of a moral network that absorbs a large part of one's energies and ambitions. . . . There is no lack of divisive ethnic conflicts in these places, whether over competing Polish and Lithuanian claims to Villnius or Hungarian irredenta vis-à-vis neighbors. But they have not flared up into violent conflicts yet because the economy has been sufficiently vigorous to provide an alternative source of belonging.[35]

I certainly do not want to claim too much here. I am not saying that the global economy's influence on culture and morality is all to the good. Enlightenment values are not all-inclusive of the set of good values. Some are ignored or omitted. I am especially cognizant of Benjamin Barber's thesis that McWorld, contrary to the view defended here, undermines democracy rather than supports it.[36] A secular materialist culture brings difficulties of its own. We have seen the dangers that come from extending the market into every corner of our lives. On a purely intellectual level see Richard Posner's discussion in *Economic Analysis of Law* (1977)[37] on the efficiency of selling babies: with an increased supply, the costs of adoption would go down, children would go to those who most wanted to have them, and the abortion rate would go down. Even if Posner's argument were correct, and there are strong considerations against it, there still seems to be something wrong in having a market in babies. At the more practical level, there are more noble reasons for nondiscrimination and the keeping of one's contracts than the fact that such behavior improves efficiency or cuts transaction costs. The values of love, friendship, and charity are more fully developed outside the commercial context. For an excellent study illustrating this point, see Richard Titmus, *The Gift Relationship* (1970).[38] Titmus shows the advantages of a system of volunteering to give blood rather than paying people to do so. A philosophical argument against the commodification of everything is provided by Elizabeth Anderson.[39] Thus, even if capitalist firms conducted business as Kantian morality requires, some moral issues surrounding capitalism would remain. However, I do find some of the unifying tendencies of international capitalism to be a positive development and I also think that international capitalism promotes diversity in many ways.

Kant and his followers are not opposed to diversity. Kant simply argues that moral claims are the kinds of claims that should be consistent and that humanity in all persons should be respected. Kant recognizes special relationships. When discussing the duty of beneficence in the *Metaphysical Principles of Virtue* he says:

> For in the wishing I may be benevolent to everyone alike; but nevertheless, in the doing, the degree may be very different according to the differences in the person loved (of whom one may concern me more than another), without violating the universality of the maxim.[40]

This point is reiterated by Barbara Herman. Herman has expanded Kantian philosophy to include the notion of normalizing and principles of moral salience. An extended discussion of Herman's rather complicated views is beyond the scope of this book. However, Herman reminds us that the use of the categorical imperative is hardly the first step in moral reflection. Kant assumed that people have been morally educated and that on the basis of moral teachings it is wrong to lie and cheat. They also know that certain kinds of action are likely to create problems, morally speaking. Herman refers to this knowledge as rules of moral salience, which she characterizes as follows:

> It is useful to think of the moral knowledge needed by Kantian agents (prior to making moral judgments) as knowledge of a kind of moral rule. Let us call them "rules of moral salience." Acquired as elements in a moral education, they structure an agent's perception of his situation so that what he perceives is a world with moral features. They enable him to pick out those elements of his circumstances or of his proposed actions that require moral attention. ... The rules of moral salience constitute the structure of moral sensitivity. They may indicate when certain sorts of actions should not be taken without moral justification.[41]

What kinds of action might be morally problematic? In living one's life certain circumstances arise in which one might wonder if one should lie, cheat, or otherwise violate the precepts of one's moral teachings. For example, if one were really hard up financially, would it be all right to borrow money with no intention of paying it back as one had promised? Does the condition of being hard up count as a legitimate exception? It is here that the categorical imperative comes into play. Kant says that we should make a maxim of our proposed exception to see if it passes the test of the categorical imperative. Thus, the categorical imperative is brought in when we are perplexed about what morality requires or when we are tempted by unusual circumstances to make an exception of ourselves. In this way the application of the categorical imperative takes place within a moral field.

To bring this discussion more to the point at issue, there is usually nothing wrong with paying special attention to our family and friends. However, if the attention is so excessive that one is never benevolent to others, then that attention has gone too far. And if we lie to benefit our family and friends we have gone too far. However, so long as our special attention to family and friends does not violate the categorical imperative, then it is morally permissible. When we wonder if we are carrying friendship too far the categorical imperative provides the test. Thus, neither Kant himself nor Kant as interpreted by contemporary scholarship thinks that there is no moral difference between family and friends and strangers.[42]

Similarly, we may recognize the bonds of religious or ethnic ties and, so long as the categorical imperative is not violated, may act partially toward those of the same religion or ethnic origin. But even if Kantian moral philosophy provides sufficient room for diversity, what can be said of international capitalism? I would argue that ethnic culture will thrive in a cosmopolitan world because human beings who see themselves as world citizens will find it easier to appreciate and tolerate the differences in cultures dissimilar to their own. In a truly cosmopolitan international marketplace, nationalism is expressed aesthetically in Greek food, Greek art, and Greek folk dances. When nationalism expresses itself politically, it is divisive and can lead to conflict. When nationalism expresses itself culturally it is easy for other nationalities to both tolerate and often appreciate and enjoy the nationalistic expression of others. I remind those who are old enough and who deplore the presence of McDonalds around the world to think of America 40 years ago. Ethnic cuisine, except for a limited number of pseudo Chinese restaurants, could only be found in major American cities and often even there in limited supply. Now, however, there is a profusion of ethnic cuisine in major American cities and there is at least limited access to such cuisine in any city in America worthy of the name. Bagels were found chiefly in New York; now they are everywhere (although arguably the only good bagels are found in New York); Americans have more opportunity to experience Eastern and African art. Buddhist and Hindu temples as well as mosques are appearing in American cities. I would certainly not claim that international capitalism is the sole or even the most important cause of these increased opportunities to experience diverse cultures. But it has certainly not hindered those opportunities and may well have aided them.

My thoughts on nationalism are consistent with this line of thought. One can celebrate one's national heritage, be proud of it, and share it with others. American cities and towns have festivals that celebrate an Italian heritage that attract many who are not Italian, that celebrate German heritage during Octoberfest that are attended by many who are not German, and of course St Patrick's day does not belong solely to the Irish. I agree with Fukuyama, who says:

> If nationalism is to fade away as a political force, it must be tolerant
> like religion before it. National groups can retain their separate

languages and sense of identity, but that identity would be expressed primarily in the realm of culture rather than politics.[43]

But after having said all of this, I would still say with Kant and fellow Enlightenment thinkers that for us to appreciate difference, we need something to bind us together. It has been the argument of this chapter that international commerce provides that bind. Commercial trade provides a reason for tolerance, the common norms of commercial morality (the morality of the marketplace) provide an experience of sameness that makes it easier to experience and appreciate cultural differences. This experience and appreciation only reinforce tolerance.

Conclusion

I have argued that the morality of the marketplace requires a certain kind of morality if a market is to be possible. To the extent that markets are international, there will be a minimum but universal market morality. I have then speculated as to what that morality would be like. I then asked whether the principles of that market would be consistent with a Kantian ethic. Even if this project is successful there is nothing inconsistent about placing additional requirements on the market. Kantian morality is permissive here. All that is required is that any particular obligations pass the tests of the categorical imperative. Certainly, the market can still be criticized and if a market practice violates the categorical imperative, that practice is wrong and should be stopped. Finally, persons have a right to criticize the market on non-Kantian grounds, i.e., that the market is too much a despoiler of the environment or that our culture is too materialistic. So my universal market morality is somewhat thin – but I hope not too thin. After all, we have shown that no capitalist country should practice bribery or discrimination. And we have shown that business people must overcome their suspicions of those from other countries and cultures so that the trust necessary for international strategic alliances can exist. Moreover, I hope the reader is convinced that Kantian moral theory has provided a major contribution to what capitalism must be like if it is to be morally justified. It does seem, after all, that if the adoption of a Kantian theory of capitalist firms could provide a universal morality for business, provide meaningful work for employees, institute firms as moral communities, and help establish a more cosmopolitan and peaceful world, Kantian capitalism will have done most everything a theory of business ethics could do. There may be other ways to achieve this end, but the Kantian theory of capitalism offers one clear blueprint. This claim may be incredibly optimistic, but then again so were Kant and the other Enlightenment thinkers.

Notes

1 Charles R. Beitz, *Political Theory and International Relations* (Princeton: Princeton University Press, 1979), pp. 181–2.

2 Terry Nardin, *Law, Morality and the Relations of States* (Princeton: Princeton University Press, 1983), p. 309.

3 R.J. Vincent, *Human Rights and International Relations* (Cambridge: Cambridge University Press, 1986), pp. 118–19.

4 Beitz, *Political Theory and International Relations*, p. 144.

5 Tom Donaldson, *The Ethics of International Business* (New York: Oxford University Press, 1989).

6 Richard DeGeorge, "International Business Ethics," *Business Ethics Quarterly* 4: 1 (January 1994), p. 3.

7 Cited in G. Pascal Zachary, "Global Growth Attains A New Higher Level That Could Be Lasting," *Wall Street Journal* March 13, 1997, p. A8.

8 Karen Pennar, "The Destructive Costs of Greasing Palms," *Business Week* December 6, 1993, pp. 133–8.

9 Catherine Yannaca-Small, "Battling International Bribery," *The OECD Observer* 192 (February–March, 1995), pp. 16–17.

10 Milton Friedman, *Capitalism and Freedom* (Chicago: University of Chicago Press, 1962), pp. 109–10.

11 R.M. Dawes, *House of Cards: Psychology and Psychotherapy Built on Myth* (New York: Free Press, 1994), p. 24.

12 This is the thesis of Francis Fukuyama's book *Trust* (New York: Free Press, 1995).

13 William C. Frederick, "The Moral Authority of Transnational Corporate Codes," *Journal of Business Ethics* 10: 3 (1991), pp. 165–77.

14 C. Langlois and B.B. Schlegelmilch, "Do Corporate Codes of Ethics Reflect National Character? Evidence from Europe and the United States,". *Journal of International Business Studies* 21 (4), 519–39.

15 Aaron Bernstein, "Sweatshop Police," *Business Week* October 20, 1997, p. 39.

16 Ibid.

17 Albert O. Hirschman, "Rival Interpretations of Market Society: Civilizing, Destructive, or Feeble," *Journal of Economic Literature* XX (December, 1982), pp. 1,463–84.

18 John Stuart Mill, *Principles of Political Economy* 1848, in *Collected Works*, vols II and III (Toronto: University of Toronto Press, 1965).

19 David Hume, "Of Refinement in the Arts," in *Essays: Moral, Political and Literary* 1752, ed. Eugene Miller (Indianapolis: Liberty Classics, 1987).

20 Adam Smith, *The Wealth of Nations*, in R. Heilbroner (ed.) *The Essential Adam Smith* (New York: W.W. Norton, 1987), p. 281.

21 Immanuel Kant, "What is Enlightenment" 1784, in *On History* (Indianapolis: Bobbs Merrill, 1963), p. 23.

22 Peter Waldman, "Israeli Business Ties With Arab Neighbors May Aid Peace Process," *Wall Street Journal* November 8, 1995, p. A1.

23 Fukuyama, *Trust*, p. 356.

24 Milton Friedman, *Capitalism and Freedom*, p. 8.

25 Friedman's argument might not hold even if we had genuine deliberative democracies. For a description of a deliberative democracy see Amy Gutmann and Dennis Thompson, *Democracy and Disagreement* (Cambridge, MA: Belknap Press, 1996). I am indebted to Tom Sorell for this point.

26 Fukuyama, *Trust*, p. 358.

27 Ibid., pp. 360, 361.

28 Anthony J.F. Reilly, quoted in *Fortune* March 26, 1990, p. 60.

29 See the various essays in Martha C. Nussbaum and Jonathan Glover (eds) *Women, Culture and Development* (Oxford: Clarendon Press, 1995).

30 Kwame Anthony Appiah, *In My Father's House: Africa in the Philosophy of Culture* (Oxford: Oxford University Press, 1992), p. 136.

31 Although Martha C. Nussbaum reports attending a conference where a French anthropologist decries the British decision to introduce the smallpox vaccine in India because it caused the demise of the cult of Sittala Devi, the goddess that could protect one from smallpox. See Nussbaum's essay "Human Capabilities, Female Human Beings," in Nussbaum and Glover, *Women, Culture and Development*, p. 65.

32 See Amartya Sen, "Capability and Well-being" and Martha Nussbaum "Non-relative Virtues: An Aristotelian Approach," both in Martha C. Nussbaum and Amartya Sen (eds) *The Quality of Life* (Oxford: Clarendon Press, 1993).

33 Onora O'Neill, "Justice, Capabilities, and Vulnerabilities," in Nussbaum and Glover, *Women, Culture and Development*, pp. 152, 149.

34 Seyla Benhabib, "Cultural Complexity, Moral Interdependence, and the Global Dialogical Community," in Nussbaum and Glover, *Women, Culture and Development*, pp. 240, 241.

35 Fukuyama, *Trust*, p. 361.

36 Benjamin R. Barber, *Jihad vs. McWorld* (New York: Ballantine Books, 1995).

37 Richard Posner, *Economic Analysis of Law* (Boston: Little, Brown, 1977).

38 R.M. Titmuss, *The Gift Relationship* (New York: Pantheon, 1971).

39 Elizabeth Anderson, *Value in Ethics and Economics* (Cambridge, MA: Harvard University Press, 1993).

40 Immanuel Kant, *The Metaphysical Principles of Virtue* 1797, in *Ethical Philosophy*, 2nd edn (Indianapolis: Hackett Publishing, 1994).

41 Barbara Herman, *The Practice of Moral Judgment* (Cambridge, MA: Harvard University Press, 1993), pp. 77, 78.

42 For a thorough discussion of these issues see Herman, *The Practice of Moral Judgment*, chapters 4 and 9.

43 Francis Fukuyama, *The End of History and the Last Man* (New York: Free Press, 1992), p. 271.

Bibliography

Argyris, Chris (1964) *Integrating the Individual and the Organization* (New York: John Wiley & Sons).

Blinder, Alan (ed.) (1990) *Paying for Productivity* (Washington DC: The Brookings Institution).

Clark, Robert C. (1985) "Agency Costs versus Fiduciary Duties" in *Principals, Agents: The Structure of Business*, ed. John W. Pratt and Richard J. Zeckhauser (Boston: Harvard Business School Press).

Greenberg, Jerald (1990) "Organizational Justice: Yesterday, Today and Tomorrow," *Journal of Management* 16, no. 2.

Herman, Barbara (1993) *The Practice of Moral Judgment* (Cambridge, Mass.: Harvard University Press).

Hill, Thomas E. Jr. (1992) *Dignity and Practical Reasoning in Kant's Moral Theory* (Ithaca, NY: Cornell University Press).

Kant, Immanuel (1963) [1775] *Lectures on Ethics* (New York: Harper Torchbooks).

Kant, Immanuel (1990) [1785] *Foundation of the Metaphysics of Morals*, 2nd edn, trans. Lewis White Beck (New York: Macmillan).

Kant, Immanuel (1993) [1788] *Critique of Practical Reason*, 3rd edn, trans. Lewis White Beck (Upper Saddle River, NJ: Prentice Hall).

Kant, Immanuel (1994) [1797] *Metaphysical Principles of Virtue*, in *Ethical Philosophy*, trans. James W. Ellington (Indianapolis: Hackett Publishing).

Korsgaard, Christine (1996) *Creating the Kingdom of Ends* (New York: Cambridge University Press).

McGregor, Douglas (1960) *The Human Side of Enterprise* (New York: McGraw Hill).

Nielsen, Richard (1996) *The Politics of Ethics* (New York: Oxford University Press).

O'Neill, Onora (1989) *Constructions of Reason* (New York: Cambridge University Press).

Ouchi, William (1981) *Theory Z* (Reading, Mass.: Addison-Wesley).

Weick, K.E. (1979) *The Social Psychology of Organizing* (New York: Random House).

Further Reading

Barber, Benjamin (1995) *Jihad vs. McWorld* (New York: Ballantine Books).

Bollier, David (1996) *Aiming Higher* (New York: American Management Association).

Bowie, Norman E. and Duska, Ronald (1990) *Business Ethics*, 2nd edn. (Englewood Cliffs, NJ: Prentice Hall).

Case, John (1995) *Open Book Management* (New York: HarperCollins Publishers).

Collins, James C. and Porras, Jerry I. (1994) *Built to Last* (New York: Harper Business).

DePree, Max (1989) *Leadership is an Art* (New York: Dell Publishing).

Donaldson, Thomas (1989) *The Ethics of International Business* (New York: Oxford University Press).

Friedman, Milton (1962) *Capitalism and Freedom* (Chicago: University of Chicago Press).

Fukuyama, Francis (1995) *Trust* (New York: The Free Press).

Handy, Charles (1996) *Beyond Certainty* (Boston: Harvard Business School Press).

Hartman, Edwin M. (1996) *Organizational Ethics and the Good Life* (New York: Oxford University Press).

Keeley, Michael (1988) *A Social Contract Theory of Organizations* (Notre Dame, Ind.: Notre Dame University Press).

O'Neill, Onora (1989) *Constructions of Reason* (New York: Cambridge University Press).

Pfeffer, Jeffrey (1998) *The Human Equation* (Boston: Harvard Business School Press).

Rawls, John (1971) *A Theory of Justice* (Cambridge, Mass.: Harvard University Press).

Reichheld, Frederick F. (1996) *The Loyalty Effect* (Boston: Harvard Business School Press).

Solomon, Robert C. (1983) *Ethics and Excellence: Cooperation and Integrity in Business* (New York: Oxford University Press).

Index